REGIONAL TRAMWAYS

SCOTLAND

REGIONAL TRAMWAYS

SCOTLAND

PETER WALLER

PEN & SWORD
TRANSPORT

Regional Tramways: Scotland

Published in 2016 by Pen & Sword Transport
an imprint of
Pen & Sword Books Ltd
47 Church Street, Barnsley, South Yorkshire, S70 2AS

© Text: Peter Waller, 2016
© Photographs: As credited

ISBN 978 1 47382 385 3

Typeset by Matthew Wharmby

Printed and Bound in India by Replika Press Pvt. Ltd

Pen & Sword Books Ltd incorporates the imprints of Pen & Sword Archaeology, Atlas, Aviation, Battleground, Discovery, Family History, History, Maritime, Military, Naval, Politics, Railways, Select, Transport, True Crime, and Fiction, Frontline Books, Leo Cooper, Praetorian Press, Seaforth Publishing and Wharncliffe.

For a complete list of Pen & Sword titles please contact
PEN & SWORD BOOKS LIMITED
47 Church Street, Barnsley, South Yorkshire, S70 2AS, England
E-mail: enquiries@pen-and-sword.co.uk
Website: www.pen-and-sword.co.uk

CONTENTS

Abbreviations

BEC:	British Electric Car Co Ltd
BET:	British Electric Traction
BTC:	British Transport Commission
EMB:	Electro-Magnetic Brake Co
ER&TCW:	Electric Railway & Tramway Carriage Works Co
GR&CW:	Gloucester Railway & Carriage Works
LRTL:	Light Railway Transport League
M&G:	Mountain & Gibson Ltd
M&T:	Maley & Taunton Ltd
PAYE:	Pay as you enter
SMT:	Scottish Motor Traction
VAMBAC:	Variable automatic multi-notch braking and control

KEY TO MAPS

Passenger lines

Lines closed before 1 January 1945

Non-passenger lines

Lines of neighbouring operators – open at 1 January 1945

Lines of neighbouring operators – closed at 1 January 1945

Passenger lines built opened after 1 January 1945

Lines under construction at 1 January 1945 – never completed

PREFACE

This is the first in a series that is intended, ultimately, to cover all the tramways of the British Isles. Its focus is on those tramway systems in Scotland that operated after 1945. However, it also provides an overview of tramway development from the horse-tram era onwards in the region. Following the introduction, individual chapters deal with each of the first-generation tramways that survived into 1945 with a map that shows the system as it existed at 1 January 1945 and a fleet list of all the trams operated after that date. Scotland also includes one second-generation tramway – Edinburgh (which finally commenced operation in 2014) – and this is also covered for the sake of completeness.

Many of the illustrations in this book were taken by my late father, Michael H. Waller, who came to know the Scottish tramways initially when a student in Dundee immediately after the Second World War, and who spent more than ten years living and working in the city and its environs. Active in the LRTL at the time and in the early days of tramcar preservation, it was a source of great regret to him that in 1956, with the closure of the Dundee system, he was forced to decline the offer of two Dundee trams for preservation. Other illustrations are drawn from the collection of Online Transport Archive (OTA); in particular, I am grateful to Barry Cross, Bob Jones, John Meredith and Hamish Stevenson, as well as to the late Marcus Eavis, Jim Joyce, Harry Luff and Phil Tatt – all of whose negatives or collections are now in the care of OTA. Martin Jenkins has been a great help in tracking down certain images and providing information. I would also like to thank George Fairley for providing information about the tramways of Edinburgh and Gavin Booth for his image of the new Edinburgh system. Every effort has been made to ensure complete accuracy; unfortunately, the records available are not always consistent and, with the passage of time, the number of those with detailed knowledge is sadly declining. Likewise every effort has been made to ensure the correct attribution of photographs. It goes without saying that any errors of fact or attribution are the author's and any corrections should be forwarded to him care of the publishers.

Peter Waller
Shrewsbury,
March 2015

INTRODUCTION

It was not until the Tramways Act of 1870 that a legal framework existed to permit the construction of street tramways. The American entrepreneur George Francis Train discovered this during the early 1860s when he endeavoured to build a number of street tramways in England. The act authorised local authorities to grant the rights to operate tramways within the local area to companies for a period of 21 years; construction of the tramway could either be undertaken by the authority and leased to the operator, or by the operator itself. The act also imposed a duty upon the operator to maintain the strip of road 18in either side of the outer running rails;

in many ways, this was the Achilles' heel of the act: at a time when roads were generally badly maintained – if they were maintained at all – the creation of this well-managed strip in the middle meant that it became available to all road users and the tram increasingly became perceived as a cause of delays to other road users as a consequence. At the end of the twenty-one-year lease, or periodically

Edinburgh & District Tramways Co Ltd took over the operation of the bulk of the horse trams operated by Edinburgh Street Tramways Co in 1894. All routes, with the exception of that to Craiglockart, were converted to cable operation between 1899 and 1901, with the final route being converted on 24 August 1907. A number of horse cars were retained after the conversion just in case of a failure in the cable system. Barry Cross Collection/Online Transport Archive

Glasgow Tramway & Omnibus Co Ltd operated almost 31½ route miles of horse trams in the city and, after July 1893, in Govan. At its peak, the fleet comprised a maximum of 233 cars. Following the corporation takeover, the last horse trams operated in Glasgow on 14 April 1902. *Barry Cross Collection/ Online Transport Archive*

thereafter, the local authority was entitled to purchase the assets of the company at a written-down value. This was a further weakness in the act in that it dissuaded the leaseholders from investing further in the business as the potential selling price would not reflect the investment undertaken. The 1870 act was subsequently amended, most notably with the Light Railways Act of 1896, but represented the basis upon which most tramways were built.

The first urban tramway in Scotland was built in Edinburgh. The standard-gauge Edinburgh Street Tramways Co first operated horse trams on 6 November 1871. Eventually the company operated a network of just under 19 route miles. In 1893 the company was split, with the routes in Edinburgh passing to Dick Kerr and, the following year, to Edinburgh & District Tramways Co. The horse cars in Edinburgh were replaced by cable trams from 1899, with the last horse cars operating on 24 August 1907. The remaining routes, in Leith, were acquired by Leith Corporation on 23 October 1904 and, following conversion to electric traction, the last horse cars operated

there on 2 November 1905. Edinburgh Street Tramways Co experimented with steam trams between 23 April 1881 and 27 October 1882, having previously experimented on three occasions, but did not persevere with this type of traction.

Outside Edinburgh, the earliest horse trams in Scotland operated in Glasgow, where Glasgow Tramway & Omnibus Co Ltd introduced its first trams operating on a gauge of 4ft 7¾in on 19 August 1872. At the expiry of the company's twenty-one-year lease on 1 July 1894, the track in the city – but not the company's trams – passed to Glasgow Corporation; the last horse trams operated on 14 April 1902. In Govan, Vale of Clyde Tramways Co commenced operation of horse trams on 16 December 1872; in 1876 powers were obtained to operate steam trams – the first act that permitted the use of mechanical traction on a street tramway – and steam-operated services commenced on 21 July 1877. Vale of Clyde Tramways Co also operated a second section, at Greenock, further west where horse trams, on the 4ft 7¾in gauge, were introduced on 7 July 1873; this section passed to Greenock & Port Glasgow Tramways Co on 7 July

Stirling & Bridge of Allan Tramways Co Ltd operated horse trams between 1874 and 1920, making it the last operator of horse trams in Scotland. Its fleet included second-hand cars, including this example that had originally been supplied to Edinburgh and which was acquired from Leith Corporation in 1905.
Barry Cross Collection/Online Transport Archive

One of the more unusual trams to operate in Scotland was the single petrol-fuelled car operated by Stirling & Bridge of Allan Tramways Co Ltd between 1913 and 1920. The tram was converted from a double-deck horse tram that the company had acquired from Edinburgh & District Tramways Co Ltd in 1902 and was fitted with a 25hp petrol engine supplied by Lanarkshire Motor Co.
Author's collection

In all there were just over 10½ route miles served by the horse trams of Aberdeen District Tramways Co, with the first route commencing operation on 31 August 1874. Cars were allocated numbers route by route; this example was one used on the service to Mannofield. Author's Collection

Dundee & District Tramway Co operated horse trams from 30 August 1877; one of the locally built double-deck cars is seen at Dalhousie Terrace in 1879. Barry Cross Collection/Online Transport Archive

1894 when Vale of Clyde's lease expired. Greenock & Port Glasgow had opened a second route in the town, again horse operated, on 29 November 1889. Horse trams continued to serve the area until 7 November 1901. Steam operation on the Vale of Clyde Tramways Co line in Govan ceased on 9 July 1893 when the line passed to the ownership of the Govan Commissioners and the lease to operate was taken on Glasgow Tramway & Omnibus Co Ltd. The company replaced steam with horse traction until 11 November 1896, when again the corporation took over, with the final horse cars operating on 9 August 1901.

In central Scotland, Stirling & Bridge of Allan Tramways Co Ltd commenced operation of the first section of its 4¹/₃ -mile long standard-gauge horse tramway on 27 July 1874; it was extended to St Ninians on 29 January 1898. This was destined to be the last horse tramway to operate in Scotland when the service ceased on 5 February 1920. This was not quite the end of trams in Stirling, however, as a single petrol-powered tram, introduced on 9 December 1913, continued to operate until the closure of the system on 20 May 1920. The petrol car was rebuilt from a second-hand horse car

acquired from Edinburgh & District in 1902.

The standard-gauge Aberdeen District Tramways Co commenced operations on 31 August 1874; the company's operations passed to the corporation on 27 August 1898 and the last horse tram in the city operated in early June 1902. Further south, horse trams appeared in Dundee under the auspices of Dundee & District Tramway Co on 30 August 1877. Taken over by the corporation on 1 June 1899, the last horse trams operated in June 1901. Back in Govan, Glasgow & Ibrox Tramways Co commenced operation of horse trams, again to a gauge of 4ft 7¾in, on 18 July 1879. The line was acquired by the Govan Commissioners in 1891 and operated by Glasgow Tramway & Omnibus Co Ltd from 28 May 1891. To the west of Glasgow, horse trams were operated by Paisley District Tramways Co between 30 December 1885 and 21 November 1903. The single route, built to a gauge of 4ft 7¾in, extended for just short of 2½ miles. In addition to the horse cars, a battery car was used experimentally in 1887. The horse trams were withdrawn to permit the electrification of the route under the auspices of Paisley District Tramways Co.

Paisley District
Tramways Co operated over a 2½-mile route between 30 December 1885 and 21 November 1903. At opening, the fleet comprised five double-deck and two single-deck cars supplied by Glasgow Tramway & Omnibus Co Ltd. One of the former is seen here; on the gable end of the building is an advert for other services that the company could offer, including 'waggonettes for hire'. Barry Cross Collection/ Online Transport Archive

In all, Rothesay Tramways Co Ltd operated 15 single-deck horse trams; 11 were open-sided but four – Nos 9-12 – were fully enclosed. This is one of the latter. The first 12 cars were delivered for the opening of the line in 1882 by the Sheffield-based company Savile Street Foundry. Barry Cross Collection/ Online Transport Archive

Two of the nine tramcars previously operated by Perth & District Tramways Co Ltd pass on 31 December 1905. The company had commenced operation with five cars, including one single-decker, on 17 September 1895 with four further double-deck cars added before the corporation took over in October 1903. Barry Cross Collection/ Online Transport Archive

One of the last horse tramways in Scotland was not in one of the great urban areas, but was built to link the Scottish Central (later Caledonian) Railway main line at Inchture station and the village of Inchture itself. The standard-gauge line opened on 1 February 1848 and was initially served by an ex-railway carriage hauled by a horse. In 1895 the Caledonian Railway built a single-deck horse tram, illustrated here, at St Rollox Works in Glasgow. The service survived until 1 January 1917; following closure, the track was salvaged and transferred to France for use on the Western Front during the First World War. Author's Collection

The most remote of Scotland's horse tramways was undoubtedly the 4ft 0in-gauge line that was built by Rothesay Tramways Co Ltd. Again just under 2½ miles in length, the first cars operated on 10 June 1892. The trams were withdrawn on 2 March 1902 to permit the conversion of the line to 3ft 6in gauge and electrification, although there was an interim service of horse trams on the relaid 3ft 6in track between 17 May 1902 and 19 August 1902 while electrification was completed. The last new urban horse tramway in Scotland was that which commenced operation in Perth on 17 September 1895; constructed to the gauge of 3ft 6in, the tramway was operated by Perth & District Tramways Co. A fleet of, ultimately, nine cars operated over 4¼ route miles. The corporation took over on 7 October 1903 and the last horse trams operated on 31 October 1905.

The last 'new' horse tramway in Scotland was, ironically, the first to have been constructed. Between Inchture, on the Dundee to Perth railway line, and Inchture village – a distance of about 1½ miles – a horse-drawn branch service was introduced on 1 February 1848 (although it did not appear in *Bradshaw* until 1867); in 1895 a new single-deck tram was constructed in Caledonian Railway's St Rollox works to operate the branch. This car remained in service until 1 January 1917 when the line closed as an economy measure during the First World War.

The first cable cars to operate in Edinburgh were introduced by Edinburgh Northern Tramways Co on 28 January 1888. The company operated 18 cars over a route that extended for just over 2½ miles. This is one of eight built by Metropolitan Railways Carriage & Wagon Co Ltd of Birmingham for the line's opening. Seating capacity was 56. Barry Cross Collection/Online Transport Archive

Edinburgh & District Tramways Co Ltd took over the horse trams of Edinburgh Street Tramways Co in 1894 and the cable cars of Edinburgh Northern Tramways Co three years later. The company converted the horse routes to cable operation, the last being completed in 1907. The corporation took over operation on the expiry of the company's lease on 1 July 1919. Barry Cross Collection/ Online Transport Archive

Edinburgh possessed the largest single cable tram system in the British Isles; the first route was operated by a subsidiary of Dick Kerr – Edinburgh Northern Tramways Co – and opened on 28 January 1888. The company's two routes passed to Edinburgh Corporation in 1897 and operation was leased to another Dick Kerr subsidiary, Edinburgh & District Tramways Co Ltd, officially from 1 July of that year. This company had earlier, in 1894, acquired the horse operations of Edinburgh Street Tramways Co. The new franchisee replaced the bulk of the routes in Edinburgh with further cable car services with the result that, at its peak, Edinburgh possessed the fourth-largest cable-car network in

the world. Part of the rationale was to avoid the use of overhead wiring in the central area; a similar desire in London led to the adoption of the conduit to provide the electric power needed for the trams. On 1 July 1919 the company's lease expired, and Edinburgh Corporation took over the operation of the cable and electric services run by the company. Work started on the conversion of the cable routes to electric traction, and all were converted between 1922 and 23 June 1923 when the last cable cars were withdrawn. A number of the ex-cable cars were converted to operate via the overhead and the last of these cars survived until shortly after the Second World War.

Edinburgh possessed a large cable-car network with a fleet of 211 trams at its peak. No 154 was one of 120 cars built by Brown Marshall during 1898 and 1899, and was later converted to operate as an electric car following the conversion of the system. Barry Cross Collection/Online Transport Archive

Dundee & District operated 13 steam tram engines; all were manufactured by Thomas Green & Son Ltd of Leeds and delivered between 1885 and 1894. No 13 is pictured with one of the 13 double-deck trailers that were built either by Milnes or by the company itself. One of the trailers is now fully restored and on display at Crich; two others survive and await restoration.
Barry Cross Collection/ Online Transport Archive

The number of steam tram operators in Scotland was relatively limited; mention has already been made of the short period in which they were operated by Edinburgh Street Tramways Co and in Govan with Vale of Clyde Tramways Co. The operator in Scotland that persisted longest with steam was Dundee & District, which introduced steam trams on 20 June 1885. The corporation acquired the company on 1 June 1899 and the last steam tram operated on 14 May 1902. The company owned 13 steam locomotives along with 13 double-deck trailers; three of the latter have been preserved, including No 21, now fully restored and on display at the National Tramway Museum, and No 2 and No 22 await restoration.

Glasgow Corporation was a pioneer of electric tramcar operation, with its first route opening on 13 October 1898. The next electric tramway was one of the more remote lines in the country. In June 1899, Great North of Scotland Railway commenced operation of the tramway at Cruden Bay, linking the hotel there with the station at Cruden Bay on the branch line from Ellon to Boddam. This 3ft 6½in-gauge route was designed to carry both passengers and freight over a line that was about two-thirds of a mile in length. Operated by two single-deck trams, built in the railway's own workshops in Aberdeen on Peckham cantilever trucks, passenger services lasted until 30 October 1932. Freight lasted longer – possibly until March 1941 – and the remains of the two cars were salvaged later for preservation, with one car being rebuilt from the parts.

Having taken over the horse routes of Aberdeen District Tramways Co, the corporation started the process of electrifying the services, with the first electric service, the Woodside route, opening on 23 December 1899. The corporation was not, however, the only operator of electric trams in the city: on 23 June 1894, Aberdeen Suburban Tramways Co opened its first section, running from Woodside to Bankhead.

A second, disconnected, route from
Mannofield to Bieldside followed on 7
July 1924. By the mid-1920s the condition
of these two routes had seriously

declined, although the corporation had
offered to acquire the routes previously.
Such was the condition of the fleet that
through-running over the corporation

The first electric cars to serve Aberdeen Corporation were eight, Nos 1-8, supplied by Brush on Brill 21E four-wheel trucks in 1899 to operate on the route to Woodside. The livery emphasised the route over which they operated. No 2 was one of four fitted with longer canopies in 1917. Author's Collection

track was banned and the two sections then simply operated as shuttle services. Services ceased on the line to Bankhead on 2 July 1927 and those to Bieldside followed just over a week later. This was not quite the end for the company lines, however, as the corporation route to Mannofield was extended by 100 yards in 1929 and that at Woodside by half a mile to the borough boundary at Scatterburn over the former company's routes.

Further south, Dundee Corporation, again having acquired the company-owned lines on 1 June 1899, set about converting the lines to electric traction. The first route, that to West Park, commenced operation on 13 July 1900, and all routes had been converted by 14 May 1902 when the last steam trams ceased operation; the final horse trams in the city had operated in June 1901. As in Aberdeen, the corporation was not the only operator of electric trams as, on 27 November 1905, Dundee, Broughty Ferry & District Tramways Co Ltd began running from Seagate in the city centre via the corporation's boundary at Craigie Terrace and Broughty Ferry to Monifieth. The company-owned section

Aberdeen Suburban Tramways Co operated two separate routes – from Woodside to Bankhead and from Mannofield to Bieldside – both of which connected with the corporation's system. One of six Brush-built double-deck cars, No 2, is pictured on Old Meldrum Road, Buckburn, on the Woodside to Bankhead section. Barry Cross Collection/Online Transport Archive

In 1900/01 Dundee Corporation received 20 open-top double-deck cars supplied by ER&TCW with Brill 21E four-wheel trucks. The first of the batch is seen when virtually new on Victoria Road heading for Fairmuir. All were fitted with top covers between 1905 and 1907, with No 21 being one of three fitted with top covers of a lowbridge design. No 21 was renumbered 33 in the late 1920s but was withdrawn early in the following decade. Author's Collection

was extended to the east slightly in 1908 but curtailed by one mile at the west in 1914 following the redrawing of Dundee's boundary. The company had running powers over corporation metals to serve the city centre and services continued through until withdrawal on 15 May 1931. The following day corporation-owned buses took over, with the corporation having acquired the company.

An opening-day photograph of Dundee, Broughty Ferry & District Tramways Co Ltd sees three of the company's fleet of trams – led by No 3 – suitably decorated to mark the opening of the line on 27 December 1905. Nos 1-12 were supplied by Brush in 1905; two of the type – Nos 1 and 2 – were fitted with open-balcony top covers in 1909. Author's Collection

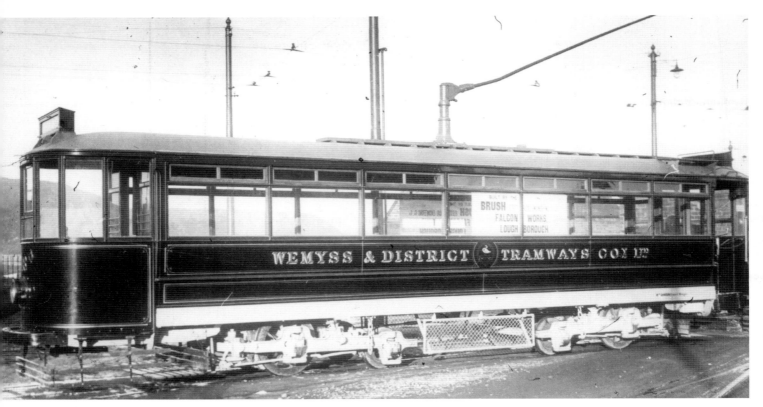

The last two trams bought new by Wemyss & District were Nos 18 and 19 that were supplied by Brush in 1925. Fitted with Brush-built maximum traction bogies, each car could accommodate 45 seated passengers. Following withdrawal, the two cars were sold in 1932 to Dunfermline Corporation as Nos 45 and 44 respectively. Barry Cross Collection/Online Transport Archive

South of the River Tay, three electric tramways all operated on the 3ft 6in gauge. The northernmost of the trio was the 7½-mile long single route operated by Wemyss & District Tramways Co Ltd. This commenced operation on 25 August 1906, running from the northernmost terminus of Kirkcaldy Corporation's system at Gallatown north along the north bank of the First of Forth as far as Leven. The company also had running powers over the 2½ miles of corporation track from Gallatown into the town centre. The line was successful, with certain sections being doubled in 1914, and with new cars being acquired until 1925 and second-hand trams until 1931, with a maximum fleet size of 21. However, bus competition grew during the 1920s and, from 1928, the operation ran at a loss. The last trams operated on 30 January 1932 and were replaced by the buses of W. Alexander & Sons. Kirkcaldy Corporation operated a network of just over six miles in length, with the first route commencing on 28 February 1903.

The system lasted until 15 May 1931; at closure, eight of the fleet's double-deck trams were sold for further use on the Wemyss & District, where they were cut down from double- to single-deck before use. The largest of the three systems between the Tay and the Forth was that of Dunfermline & District Tramways Co; this commenced operation on 2 November 1909 and ultimately extended over a network of almost 18½ miles, with the last extension being completed in 1913 and with a maximum fleet of 45 cars. During the 1920s one of the longer routes was doubled and some of the line transferred to roadside reservations. Further extensions were proposed but never constructed, although one route was extended by 100 yards in 1930. The company's acquisition by Scottish Motor Traction in 1935 sealed the fate of the tramway, although the first route had been converted to bus operation in 1931. The last trams operated on 4 July 1937, being replaced by the buses of W. Alexander & Sons.

Kirkcaldy Corporation operated a system of just over six route miles between 1903 and 1931. The fleet comprised 26 open-top double-deck trams. No 6, seen here on Kirkcaldy High Street, was one of ten supplied by Milnes in 1902 with Milnes-built Pressed Steel four-wheel trucks. At closure, eight of the corporation fleet was sold to Wemyss & District for further use.
Barry Cross Collection/Online Transport Archive

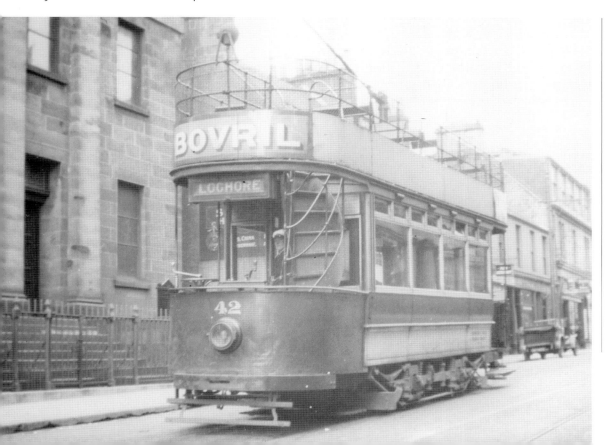

In all, UEC supplied 43 open-top double-deck trams to Dunfermline & District Tramways Co between 1909 and 1917; No 42, seen here, was one of the last batch, Nos 29-43, that was supplied during the First World War. Seating capacity was 56. This batch was the only one supplied with trucks also built by UEC; the remaining 28 were fitted with Brill 21E four-wheel trucks.
Barry Cross Collection/Online Transport Archive

In 1910 Edinburgh & District inaugurated the first electric trams to serve the Scottish capital. Four cars — Nos 28, 38, 64 and 74 — were built by G. F. Milnes & Co Ltd on Brill 22E bogies for use on the Slateford route. The quartet passed to Edinburgh Corporation where all were converted to covered-top four-wheelers and renumbered 229, 230, 268 and 269. No 28, as No 229, was withdrawn for scrap in 1934. Barry Cross Collection/Online Transport Archive

With the Nelson Monument in the background, Edinburgh Corporation No 154 is about to take the curve from Waterloo Place into Leith Street at the east end of Princes Street. No 154 was originally a cable car — see page 15 — but was converted to operate on the city's electrified routes. It was to survive until 1927 and, following the usual Edinburgh arrangement, the top deck of the withdrawn car, which was much newer than the lower deck, was reused on a new lower saloon that was given the same number as the withdrawn cable car. Barry Cross Collection/ Online Transport Archive

South of the Firth of Forth, the first electric trams were introduced to the capital by Edinburgh & District Tramways Co Ltd when the company's route to Slateford opened on 8 June 1910, but the city's cable network dominated until after the corporation took over the company's lines on 1 July 1919. After this, the cable network was progressively converted to electric operation with a number of the more recent cable cars converted to operate using electricity; the final

THE REGISTER, EDINBURGH.

Leith Corporation operated electric trams between 1905 and November 1920, when operation was taken over by Edinburgh Corporation. No 31 was one of three cars, Nos 31-33, built by UEC in 1905 on Brill 21E trucks. The trio became Nos 261-63 following the Edinburgh takeover, and they were to survive in service until 1932 (No 261) and 1933 (Nos 262/63). Barry Cross Collection/Online Transport Archive

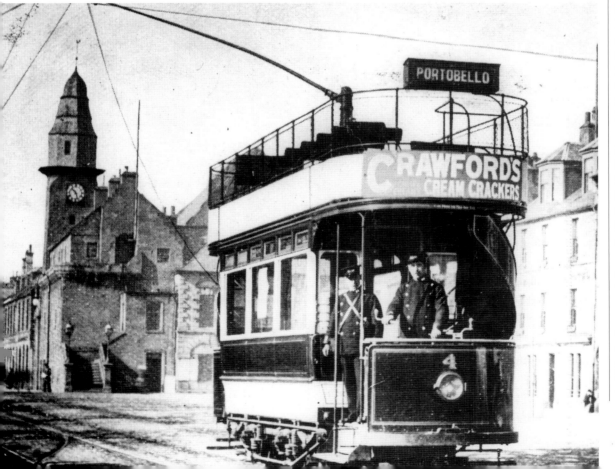

Musselburgh & District Electric Light & Traction Co Ltd operated in total 22 trams. The first 16 were all delivered new by UEC or Brush between 1904 and 1909; the remaining six were all second-hand acquisitions from Sheffield Corporation. No 4, seen here in 1905, was one of the original ten UEC-built open-top cars delivered for the line's opening in 1904. Fitted with BEC SB60 trucks, all ten were fitted with top covers within five years of delivery. Barry Cross Collection/Online Transport Archive

The 4ft 0in-gauge tramway operated by Falkirk & District Tramways Co had originally been operated with open-top trams, some of which were supplied by a French company. Between 1929 and 1931 14 new single-deck cars were delivered – Nos 1-10 in 1929/30 and Nos 13-16 in 1931. These were all built by Brush and fitted with Brush-built Burnley bogies. Destined for a short life, all were withdrawn for scrap following closure in 1936, although the body of No 14 was secured for preservation and is now restored using ex-Glasgow subway trucks and is owned by Falkirk Museums. Barry Cross Collection/Online Transport Archive

cable cars operated in the city on 23 June 1923. Following the conversion of the final cable routes, the corporation continued to extend its network until the Second World War, with the final extension – of the Corstorphine route to Maybury – opening on 14 February 1937. If war had not started, there would have been further extensions; work was authorised on 6 January 1938 on the route to Crewe Toll and construction work started, after a delay, the following year. With the onset of war, construction was suspended. Edinburgh's port was Leith and a separate, but linked, electric tramway served the town from 18 August 1905. Leith Corporation had acquired the horse operation within its boundaries on 23 October 1904 and the last horse tram operated on 2 November

1905. Leith Corporation's network was taken over by Edinburgh Corporation on 2 November 1920. Further to the east, and terminating close to the Joppa terminus of Leith Corporation, were the electric trams of Musselburgh & District Electric Light & Traction Co Ltd. The company operated a single route from Joppa to Port Seton, a distance of about 6½ miles. The service commenced on 12 December 1904; initially there was no connection with the corporation line at Joppa, but this was rectified in 1920 and through-running to central Edinburgh commenced. The company continued operating until 1 March 1928 when, with the exception of workmen's services, all trams were withdrawn; the surviving operations ceased on 31 March 1928. Thereafter the corporation continued to operate

H ROAD. SCONE 650.

the Joppa to Levenhall section, finally purchasing this section on 7 May 1931.

To the west of Edinburgh, the town of Falkirk possessed a 4ft 0in-gauge tramway that extended over almost eight miles and commenced operation on 21 October 1905. Operated by Falkirk & District Tramways Co, the initial batch of 15 cars were unusual in that they were supplied by a French manufacturer – the *Compagnie Générale de Construction* of St Denis. Although the company acquired 14 new single-deck trams between 1929 and 1931 along with five second-hand cars in 1933, the purchase of the company by Scottish Motor Traction resulted in the tramway being converted to bus operation on 21 July 1936.

Slightly further to the north was Perth; here the corporation, having acquired the horse cars of Perth & District Tramways Co Ltd on 7 October 1903, converted the line to electricity, with the new electric cars operating from 31 October 1905. A fleet of 12 cars operated over some five miles of route until replaced by corporation-owned buses on 19 January 1929.

Moving to the west, two tramways served Ayrshire. The first to open, on 26 September 1901, was that serving Ayr. Operated by Ayr Corporation Tramways, the standard-gauge system comprised one long route with a branch that served the racecourse. The total length was just under 6½ route miles and in all some 30 trams, including one works car, were owned. The last trams, two second-hand cars acquired from Dumbarton, entered service in 1928. The demise came when Scottish Motor Traction offered to buy the tramway in 1931; despite significant work undertaken on the system, the corporation agreed to the sale and the trams were replaced by company-owned buses on 1 January 1932. The trams operated for the last time on 31 December, although the two ex-Dumbarton cars were sold for further service to South Shields. Further east the 4¼-mile standard-gauge tramways of Kilmarnock Corporation Tramways commenced operation on 10 December 1904. The system comprised a single north-south route with a branch to the east serving

Perth No 5, seen here on the route out to Scone (where the system's sole depot was located), was one of 12 cars delivered for the opening of the system in 1905. All were supplied by Scottish-based Hurst Nelson and fitted with Hurst Nelson-built trucks. These 12 were the only electric trams operated by the corporation and were replaced by buses in 1929. Author's collection

Ayr Corporation operated effectively a two-route system with some 30 cars owned during its life. No 14 was one of six open-top cars delivered by Hurst Nelson on the same company's four-wheel cantilever trucks. In the late 1920s, this car was retrucked, receiving a second-hand truck from either another Ayr car or one acquired from Kilmarnock. Barry Cross Collection/Online Transport Archive

Kilmarnock Corporation operated electric trams between 1904 and 1926. In all, 14 trams were employed, the last of which, No 14, one of two open-balcony cars supplied by Hurst Nelson on Hurst Nelson 21E four-wheel trucks, is recorded on Kilmarnock High Street. Barry Cross Collection/Online Transport Archive

Hurlford over which operated a fleet of 14 double-deck cars. The first abandonment, the route to Hurlford, occurred in 1924 with the remainder of the system closing on 3 May 1926 as a result of the General Strike. The trams were replaced initially by corporation-owned buses.

On the south bank of the Firth of Clyde, the 4ft 7¾in-gauge horse trams of Greenock & Port Glasgow Tramways Co were acquired by BET in May 1900 and the new owner converted the single route, which was just under 7½ miles in length, to electric traction. The electric cars commenced operation on 3 October 1901 with the last horse trams running on 7 November of the same year. In all some 48 trams were operated, including two acquired second-hand from Rothesay Tramways Co Ltd in 1915. The last trams operated on 15 July 1929, with the company having decided not to renew its lease. Company-owned buses

replaced the trams. Across the Firth, on the north side, there was a link between the Glasgow Corporation terminus at Dalmuir with Balloch (a distance of more than ten miles), courtesy of Dumbarton Borough & County Tramways Co Ltd. The company was a subsidiary of the Electricity Supply Corporation Ltd, which retained ownership until 31 December 1907, and its first routes, constructed to the Glasgow standard gauge of 4ft 7¾in, opened on 20 February 1907. The long route to Balloch finally opened throughout on 25 June 1908; a short branch to Jamestown opened on 24 February 1909. With its long single-track sections, the tramway found bus competition to be disastrous, and the final trams operated on 3 March 1928. On closure, two of the 32 trams were sold for further service in Ayr.

Promoted by Paisley District Tramways Co, a network of more than 18 route miles

Six cars, Nos 1-6, were supplied to Dumbarton Burgh & County Tramways while in the ownership of the Electric Supply Corporation. The six cars, of which No 4 is seen here, were built in 1907 by Brush and fitted with M&G 21EM trucks. The cars were fitted with balcony tops from new. The next batch of cars – Nos 7-26 supplied by UEC the following year – were open-top when new, although three were subsequently fitted with second-hand top-deck covers. Barry Cross Collection/Online Transport Archive

In 1904 BEC supplied a batch of 39 open-top cars to Paisley District Tramways Co for the opening of the system. Nos 1-29 were fitted with Brush AA trucks and could seat 55 passengers. Along with most of the Paisley fleet, No 23 passed to the ownership of Glasgow Corporation on 1 August 1923. No 23 was one of 17 ex-Paisley cars – Nos 9-19, 22-24/27, 37/38 – that were cut down to single-deck for use on the Duntocher route. Two of these – Glasgow Nos 1016/17 – survive in preservation.
Barry Cross Collection/ Online Transport Archive

A commercial postcard franked on 22 April 1910 shows Airdrie & Coatbridge Tramways Co No 8, one of a batch of 12 delivered by Brush for the system's opening in 1904. The cars were fitted with Brush AA trucks and accommodated 56 seated passengers. All 12 passed to Glasgow Corporation, as Nos 1073-1084, on 31 December 1921 and remained open-top through their career; the last were withdrawn in January 1932. Barry Cross Collection/Online Transport Archive

of 4ft 7¾in-gauge line serving Paisley, Renfrew and district was constructed. The first route, from Hawkhead Road to Paisley Cross, opened on 13 June 1904. Adjoining the larger Glasgow system at a number of locations, the Paisley network was taken over by Glasgow Corporation on 1 August 1923, which acquired the company's fleet of trams plus depots at Renfrew, Barrhead and Elderslie (where the company's workshops were located). The bulk of the ex-Paisley network, with the

exceptions of the route to Abbotsinch and the westernmost part of the Kilbarchan route beyond Ferguslie (both of which were abandoned in the early 1930s), survived into the post-1945 era. The Paisley company was not the only one to be acquired by Glasgow Corporation. BET sponsored the construction of a 4ft 7¾in-gauge tramway in Airdrie and Coatbridge with the first section of the company's network opening on 8 February 1904. On 30 September 1920, Airdrie & Coatbridge Tramways Co was

The Lanarkshire Tramways Co operated over almost 28½ route miles of 4ft 7¾in gauge and employed some 92 passenger cars during its 28-year life. No 13 was one of the first batch of 25, Nos 1-25, delivered for the system's opening in 1903. Built by BEC on BEC SC60 trucks, all were reconstructed in the company's workshops between 1912 and 1923 when they were fitted with Hurst Nelson trucks. Barry Cross Collection/Online Transport Archive

acquired by the two towns and operation was transferred to Airdrie & Coatbridge Tramway Trust the next day. This arrangement lasted until 31 December 1921 when the system, which was just over 3½ miles in length, was sold to Glasgow Corporation. The two networks were linked on 30 December 1923 by the opening of a new high-speed tramway between Langloan and Baillieston.

A further system was physically linked to the lines of Glasgow Corporation, but was never in corporation ownership. This was the extensive – almost 28½ route miles – system operated by Lanarkshire Tramways Co centred on Motherwell. The first section of the 4ft 7¾in-gauge system, linking Hamilton, Motherwell and Wishaw, opened on 22 July 1903; this had been promoted by Hamilton, Motherwell & Wishaw Light Railways

Co but the company's name was soon changed to Lanarkshire Tramways Co. Although acquiring new trams as late as 1925, the network suffered from significant sections of single track and competition in the 1920s weakened it financially. The last trams operated on 14 February 1931 and were replaced by the buses of SMT.

There was one remaining electric tramway in Scotland and this was perhaps the most remote of all – the 3ft 6in-gauge route operated by Rothesay Tramways Co Ltd on the Isle of Bute. The company had constructed a 4ft 0in-gauge horse tramway but BET acquired the company with the intention of converting the line to electric power. In order to operate with double track throughout, the line was relaid to 3ft 6in gauge with the last of the 4ft 0in-gauge horse trams operating on 2 March

In this pre-First World War view, three of Rothesay Tramways Co's fleet of single-deck combination cars are visible. This is the view from the Guildford Square terminus looking towards the north. Author's collection

1902. Following reconstruction, a horse service was reintroduced on 17 May 1902, which operated until 19 August 1902 when the electric trams were introduced. In 1905 the route was extended at the western end to Ettrick Bay, resulting in a line that extended just over 4¾ route miles. Rothesay was a popular holiday destination and the trams were heavily used during the summer months; the state of the economy following the Wall Street Crash of 1929 led to the decision to cease the winter service in January 1931. That same year the company was acquired by SMT; the single-deck trams survived in service until 30 September 1936 when they were replaced by company-owned buses.

Thus, by the outbreak of war in September 1939, the number of passenger tramways active in Scotland had been reduced to those serving the major cities of Aberdeen, Dundee, Edinburgh and Glasgow.

ABERDEEN

The northernmost of all surviving tramways in the British Isles in 1945, Aberdeen was widely regarded during the immediate post-war years as one of the most secure systems in the country. Apart from two route closures in 1931 – the routes to Torry and to Duthie Park on 28 February and 30 May respectively – the tramway was intact. Indeed, during the 1930s, the policy had been to invest in the system, with work starting in 1937, for example, on a direct route from the city centre to Sea Beach and, in 1938, on the extension of the Woodside route over the route of the closed Aberdeen Suburban Tramways

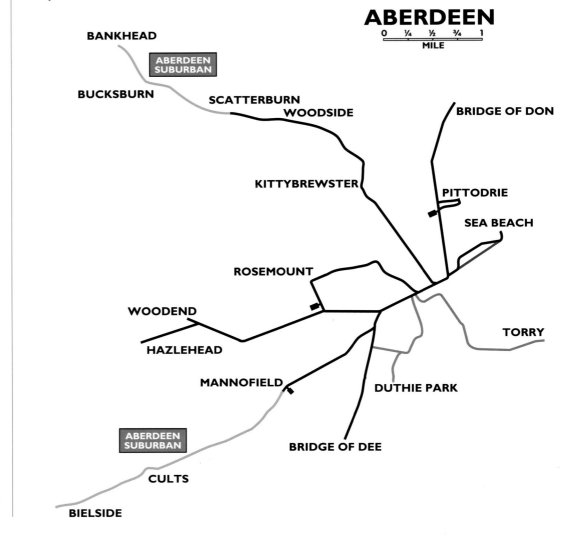

Map of the Aberdeen network as at 1945.

Co. In addition, new and second-hand trams had been acquired, most notably 18 cars from Nottingham in 1936 and four new streamlined cars in 1940.

That the tram was still seen as ideal for Aberdeen was stressed in an article written by the convener of the Transport Committee, Councillor William Collins, and published in the *Evening Express* on 30 March 1945, as well as by the rejection by the Transport Committee on 7 June 1945, and by the full council on 21 July 1945 of a proposal made by Councillor Sutherland either to convert one route or the entire system to bus operation. Moreover, the general manager, Alfred Smith, was empowered to purchase a further 20 new double-deck trams, and there were hopes that the construction of the alternative route to Sea Beach, delayed by the war, would be resumed. Further trams were acquired in late 1946 when it was agreed to bid for a number of the 'Pilcher' cars then being withdrawn in Manchester.

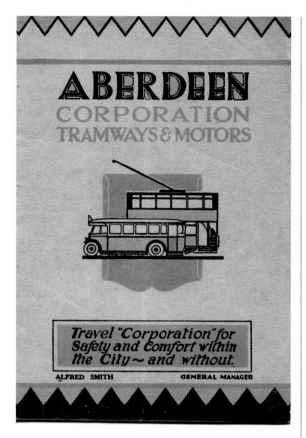

ABERDEEN CORPORATION TRAMWAYS & MOTORS

Travel "Corporation" for Safety and Comfort within the City ~ and without.

ALFRED SMITH   GENERAL MANAGER

Issued in 1940 by Aberdeen Corporation Transport Department, this booklet gave readers a guide to travelling round the city by public transport. The impact of war was real: page 2 included a 'War Emergency Notice' that read: 'Wherever reference is made to the BEACH in any of the Tours in this Booklet the CORPORATION OF ABERDEEN desires to inform passengers that a certain part of the BEACH is closed to Vehicular Traffic. Tours in that direction are therefore slightly curtailed.'
Author's Collection

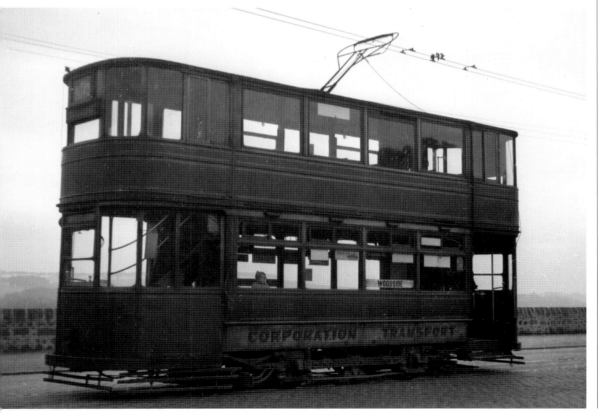

Ex-Nottingham No 15, one of 18 acquired second-hand in 1936, stands at the Woodside terminus in 1947.
Michael H. Waller

The penultimate of a batch of nine cars delivered between 1926 and 1931, No 123 is pictured at the Mannofield terminus in 1947. Michael H. Waller

One of the two wartime four-wheel cars, No 140, heads along Castle Street on 29 June 1948. This side view shows to good effect the roller platform doors that were fitted to these cars. Michael H. Waller

Aberdeen was one of two Scottish operators to acquire 'Pilcher' cars second-hand from Manchester. No 270, seen here being transported north over Beattock, was destined to become Aberdeen No 48.
Michael H. Waller

One of the 20 post-war streamline cars is pictured at the Bridge of Dee terminus on 1 April 1950.
Michael H. Waller

Pictured at the Bridge of Don terminus is the first of the 14 ex-Manchester Corporation 'Pilcher' cars, No 39, acquired in 1947 and 1948; this had originally been Manchester No 121.
Michael H. Waller

The first route to be converted to bus operation after the Second World War was that to Mannofield, which succumbed in May 1951. A year before, on 1 April 1950, one of the ex-Manchester cars, No 50, stands at the terminus.
Michael H. Waller

Although new and second-hand trams were on order, approval was granted in early 1947 for the conversion of the Mannofield route to bus operation with trams being retained elsewhere; commentators at the time, however, noted that the conversion would not be practical for some time as it required the purchase of new buses – and these were not plentiful in the post-war years – and that any new vehicles would be needed to replace some of the corporation's existing bus fleet. That the route's demise was not imminent was demonstrated by the fact that sections were relaid during the late 1940s.

By early 1949 the first of the new streamlined trams was delivered to the

corporation's workshops for final assembly and the first two – No 19 and No 20 – had entered service. By the summer the first ten were in service and the remainder had been delivered. The new trams were seen on all routes with the exception of that to Woodside owing to the single track and loops section on narrow St Nicholas Street. Also during the summer some 3½ miles of track on the Woodside route was relaid at a cost of £26,696. Early 1950 also saw further investment with the extension of the depot at Queen's Cross, which was required as a result of space problems at King Street following the arrival of Nos 19-39, plus the possible need to rehouse trams from Mannofield depot should the Mannofield route close.

The death, announced in the January 1951 edition of *Modern Tramways*, of Baillie William Collins, convenor of the Transport Committee, was a loss to the backers of Aberdeen's trams as he had been a staunch supporter of the system over many years. It was probably coincidental that the long-threatened conversion of the Mannofield route took place on 3/4 May 1951. The abandonment of the service to Mannofield resulted in the withdrawal of the last of the ex-Nottingham cars.

Another of the tramway's supporters, Alfred Smith, departed to be replaced in April 1953 by F. Y. Frazer, who had previously been general manager at Lincoln (an all-bus fleet). The tide was, perhaps, now turning against the tram in Aberdeen.

From 26 October 1953 to April 1954 the service to Sea Beach was suspended on weekdays; this was designed to conserve the track over the route, and to save the cost of vehicles and crew. By the early 1950s, the finances of the Transport Department had deteriorated; in 1952/53, for example, the trams made a profit of £8,667 but the buses lost £43,539. Fare increases and cost savings were the order of the day. In March 1954 tram services over the Rosemount Circles, routes 5 and 6, which had been losing £6,000 per annum, were reduced during off-peak hours and a new bus service to Mastrick was rerouted to cover some of the route. On 24 June 1954 the Transport Committee decided that, to reduce the losses yet further, the Rosemount Circle routes were to be converted to bus operation. The route was to be converted to bus operation overnight on 2/3 October 1954; the closure was marked by the operation of the preserved horse tram No 1.

One of the ex-Nottingham cars, No 13, stands in Castle Street on 24 January with a service to Sea Beach. The conversion of the Mannofield service saw the last of these cars withdrawn from service. Michael H. Waller

Aberdeen Corporation introduced the Ultimate ticketing system in 1952 to replace the earlier TIM system. This is an example from the earliest Ultimate tickets issued by Aberdeen Corporation Transport. Author's Collection

In August 1952 a line-up of six trams, headed by 1920-built open-balcony No 87, stand on the loop serving the football ground at Pittodrie. R. W. A. Jones/Online Transport Archive (AN42)

Brush-built No 131 awaits its next duty on route 6 – the Rosemount Circle – on Castle Street on 1 April 1950. Note the coloured route board. Michael H. Waller

Tracklifting started on the Rosemount route on 29 August 1955.

With the tramway network now reduced, the Transport Committee voted on 31 January 1955 to accept a report from the new general manager that the entire network be converted to bus operation by the end of 1958. By the summer of 1955, following the earlier conversions, the Aberdeen fleet numbered 71 passenger cars (Nos 19-38, 40/41/43/45/47-49, 50/52, 62/63, 99-108/11-24/26-41) plus three works cars (Nos 4A, 76 and 87).

The next conversion was the route

Aberdeen No 99 is seen at the terminus of the Woodside route on 28 May 1955; this route was converted to bus operation six months later. Michael H. Waller

One of the 1929 batch of Brush-built cars, No 134, loads at Sea Beach in July 1955. John B. McCann/Online Transport Archive

to Woodside, which succumbed to bus operation on 27/28 November 1955, with the last tram to Woodside being No 108. The conversion saw 15 buses replace 17 trams; the following were withdrawn as a result of the closure: Nos 47, 50, 116-22/30. The estimated cost of removing the tramway infrastructure plus reinstating the road was £180,000.

In June 1956 the summer all-day service to Sea Beach was reinstated, but the tram fleet continued to shrink with the withdrawal of the last of the ex-Manchester 'Pilcher' cars; the bodies of three of these were used as staff rooms at the bus garage. On 22 September it was announced that the Hazlehead-Sea Beach route was to be abandoned during the winter of 1956/57 as a result, it was claimed by the City Engineer, of the poor condition of the track. This closure was 12 months earlier than originally envisaged. The Sea Beach service reverted to its winter schedule on 29 September 1956, shuttling to and from Castle Street; however, as a result of the Suez Crisis, an all-day service was reintroduced using one tram on 17 December 1956 with the intention that this would operate until the problems with fuel supplies ended.

Following the reduction in the Sea Beach service, on 7/8 October the Hazlehead extension beyond Woodend of route No 4 was converted to bus operation; this was to permit the conversion of the tram reservation into a roadway for the replacement buses. A further ten trams — Nos 99-101/04/13/14/26/28/29/40 — were withdrawn for scrap at this stage with the fleet now reduced to 41 passenger cars plus the three works cars. The Woodend route was converted to bus operation on 17/18 November 1956 and Sea Beach succumbed finally on 13 March 1957 as a result of the failure of an underground feeder cable. The track at Sea Beach did, however, have a final role in the history of Aberdeen's trams: on withdrawal the last trams were taken there to be scrapped by Bird's of Stratford.

At the end of 1957 it was announced that the trams had lost £54,159 in the previous year as opposed to a profit of £84,447 on the buses. It was pointed out that the sole remaining tram route was carrying all the debt charges previously carried by the whole tram network and that these costs would fall onto the buses once the last trams were withdrawn. On 23 January 1958 the Transport Committee

The last of the batch of ten cars built by Brush in 1925, No 115, stands at the terminus at Hazlehead on 28 May 1955. The third track was used by extra cars at times of peak demand.
Michael H. Waller

approved 3 May 1958 as the system's final day. In order to accommodate the additional buses required, the south wing of King Street depot was demolished in early 1958; this also resulted in the destruction of the three remaining 'Pilcher' bodies. All 41 surviving passenger cars were offered for scrap post-closure; the 41 were significantly more than was required for the service and many were in store at Queen's Cross at closure.

Passengers queue to board Aberdeen No 73 at the Woodend terminus in August 1952. No 73 was one of six open-balcony cars originally supplied by the local company, J. T. Clark, in 1913. R. W. A. Jones/Online Transport Archive (AN24)

The last day of tramway service in Aberdeen: one of the post-war streamlined cars, No 21, awaits departure from the Bridge of Don terminus on 3 May 1958. At closure, the fleet numbered 41. This was more than required for service but the corporation had to retain two fleets as the bogie streamliners were often replaced in severe winter conditions by the Standards.
Michael H. Waller

The crowds gather in Castle Street, central Aberdeen, as the closure is marked by a procession of trams. Visible in the distance is the preserved horse tram whilst closest to the camera is streamlined No 32.
Michael H. Waller

To mark the closure of the tramway system in May 1958, Aberdeen Corporation produced a small commemorative booklet marking 60 years of municipal operation.
Author's Collection

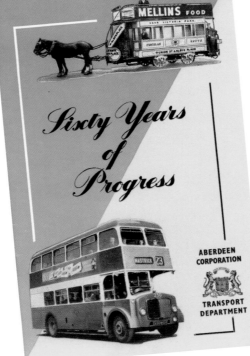

Final closure came on 3 May 1958 with No 20 providing the last public service on the Bridge of Don section. Of the 20 postwar streamlined cars, only 11 – Nos 19-24/26/29, 32/36/37 – survived in service until the end with the remainder used to provide spare parts.

Six passenger cars – Nos 108/35, 32/33/37/36 (in that order with No 36 accommodating the official party – made the official last journey to Bridge of Dee and return, being joined by the preserved horse tram for part of the journey. As if to emphasise the final demise, No 103 was derailed in King Street depot after the ceremony concluded. With indecent haste the final trams were despatched to Sea Beach where Bird's had completed the dismantling within a week; no Aberdeen electric tram was preserved.

Aberdeen Depots

Aberdeen was served by a number of depots post-war. King Street, situated on route north to Bridge of Don, close to the loop serving the football ground at Pittodrie, was the location both of a running shed and the corporation's main workshops, where the bodies of the trams constructed by the corporation itself were completed. This depot survived until the final closure of the tramway system on 3 May 1958. Other depots were: Mannofield, one of two depots close to the terminus at Mannofield – the other being one owned by Aberdeen Suburban Tramways Co that closed in 1927; the corporation depot was closed on 5 March 1951 with the conversion of the Mannofield service to bus operation. Woodside, located on the Great Northern Road close to Don Street railway station on the Aberdeen-Inverness line, retained a tram allocation until 26 November 1955 when the route to Woodside was converted to bus operation. Queens Cross was one of two depots, East and West, built for the tramways between Queens Cross and Rosemount; whereas the East Depot closed in 1900, the West Depot survived until 7 October 1956, at the same time as services were withdrawn on the Hazlehead route, having been slightly extended in 1951.

Aberdeen Closures

3 March 1951	2 – Mannofield
2 October 1954	5, 6 – Rosemount Circle
26 November 1955	7 – Woodside
7 October 1956	4 – Hazlehead-Woodend
17 November 1956	4 – Woodend
13 March 1957	3 – Sea Beach
3 May 1958	1 – Bridge of Don-Bridge of Dee

On the occasion of an LRTL tour on 17 August 1950, open-balcony No 81, one of a trio fitted with Brill 79E four-wheel trucks, is seen at the main depot and workshops at King Street.
Michael H. Waller

Aberdeen Fleet

1-18

Bought second-hand in 1936, this batch was originally supplied to Nottingham in 1926/27 as Nos 181-99 (the 19th car was also acquired as a source of spares). However, the trams were brought up in three sections and so there is no correlation between the numbers in Nottingham and those allocated in Aberdeen. The trams had English Electric bodies on Peckham P22 trucks with the exception of Nos 14/14/18, which were on Brill 21E trucks. The batch was withdrawn from service between 1949 and 1951; No 18 was retained for use as a works car following withdrawal in 1950.

19-38

Aberdeen's last new trams were 20 streamlined cars with bodies built by R. Y. Pickering & Co of Wishaw on EMB Lightweight bogies. The trams were slightly modified in 1954/55 when fitted with power-operated platform doors and the seating capacity increased by two to 76; the cars originally needed two conductors to be operated, but the alteration meant that the doors could be operated by the driver, thus allowing the second conductor to be removed. This modification resulted in an annual saving of £1,050 in staff costs. The whole batch was withdrawn in 1958 when less than ten years old.

39-52

Aberdeen was one of four operators that took advantage of Manchester's policy of tramway abandonment in the late 1940s to acquire a number of the last new trams that Manchester had acquired – the 'Pilcher' cars supplied between 1930 and 1932 originally. Aberdeen took 14; these had been Nos 121, 483, 420, 671, 161, 610, 274, 669, 141, 270, 106, 225, 510 and 502 in Lancashire. Fitted with bodies built in Manchester's own workshops on Peckham P35 four-wheel trucks, they entered service in Aberdeen in 1948. All were withdrawn from service during 1955 and 1956.

On 24 January 1949 No 2, one of the batch of trams acquired second-hand from Nottingham in 1936, is seen on Castle Street. Alongside is No 89, one of the batch of 12 open-balcony cars supplied during 1920 and 1921. Note the coloured route blind.
Michael H. Waller

The last wholly new trams acquired by Aberdeen were the 20 streamlined cars, Nos 19-38, that were built by R. Y. Pickering & Co Ltd of Wishaw in 1949. No 32 is seen at the Bridge of Dee terminus on 3 May 1958. It is a tragedy that these cars survived less than a decade in service and that none survived into preservation. Michael H. Waller

Although showing route No 1 – from Bridge of Don to Bridge of Dee – No 48, one of the batch of 14 'Pilcher' cars acquired second-hand from Manchester during 1947 and 1948, stands at Mannofield, outside the depot, on 3 March 1951. Michael H. Waller

33-56(i)

Originally supplied as open-top and open-platform cars in 1903, this batch was built with bodies supplied by Dick Kerr on Brill 21E trucks. All were later fitted with top covers and platform vestibules. All were withdrawn by 1950 with No 54 being converted to railgrinder No 4A on withdrawal in 1948. This survived in works service until 1958.

57-63/66/67

These nine trams were built as open-balcony cars in 1919 (Nos 66/67) and 1922/23 (remainder) with bodies built in the corporation's workshops. All were initially fitted with Brill 21E four-wheel trucks but these were replaced by Peckham P35s. Nos 57-61/66/67 were built from new with lower-deck vestibules, and Nos 57-61 were fully

enclosed in 1936. Nos 62/63 were delivered as fully enclosed from new. The first to be withdrawn was No 66 in 1951, followed by No 67 in 1953. Nos 57-61 were withdrawn during 1953/54 and the remaining two survived until 1958.

72-77

Supplied in 1913 with open-balcony bodies built by J. T. Clark on Brill 21E four-wheel trucks, this was a batch of PAYE trams rebuilt as standard vehicles with platform vestibules in 1913. The bulk of the batch was later fitted with Peckham P35 trucks. Withdrawal came between 1952 and 1955. No 73 was preserved on withdrawal in 1954, only to be scrapped the following year. No 76 was converted to works use following withdrawal in 1952 and survived until 1958.

No 55, one of the surviving BEC-built cars that were delivered as open-top during 1902 and 1903, is pictured at Mannofield in 1947. All of this type were withdrawn by 1950 as the second-hand ex-Manchester 'Pilchers' and the new Pickering-built trams were delivered. Michael H. Waller

During 1922 and 1923 Aberdeen constructed five open-balcony cars, Nos 57-61, that were the last to be built for the corporation in this style. All were delivered with enclosed lower vestibules and were rebuilt as fully enclosed in 1936. No 61 is seen at Queens Cross on 24 January 1949. Michael H. Waller

The local company of J. T. Clark constructed one batch of trams for Aberdeen, the six open-balcony cars, Nos 72-77, that were delivered in 1913. These were originally built for PAYE but were rebuilt with conventional vestibules in 1923. No 77 is pictured at the Bridge of Don terminus on 24 January 1949. Michael H. Waller

One of the 1914 batch of open-balcony cars, No 79, is seen at the Woodend terminus in August 1952 shortly before its withdrawal. R. W. A. Jones/ Online Transport Archive (AN23)

78-83
Dating originally to 1914, this batch of trams was supplied with Brush open-balcony bodies on M&G 21EM four-wheel trucks. Designed as PAYE trams, they were rebuilt as standard vehicles with platform vestibules in 1913. The batch was subsequently fitted with Peckham P35 trucks with Nos 81-83 later fitted with Brill 79E trucks. All were withdrawn between 1949 and 1953.

No 96, seen at Queens Cross on 24 January 1949, was one of 12 open-balcony cars supplied during 1920 and 1921 that were vestibuled from new. Never fitted with enclosed balconies, all were withdrawn between 1950 and 1953. Michael H. Waller

The unique experimental high-speed tram, No 99, of 1923 seen at Bridge of Don on 24 January 1949. This car was originally fitted with a Brill 21E truck, but this had been replaced by a Peckham P35 by the date of this photograph. Michael H. Waller

84-86

This batch was supplied in 1918/19 and was partly constructed from parts salvaged from earlier cars. The bodies were built in the corporation's workshops on Brill 21E trucks. Withdrawn from passenger service in 1932/33, the three cars were used as salt cars thereafter, after having been fitted with folding windscreens.

87-98

Built in 1920/21 as open-balcony cars, this batch of four-wheel cars was fitted with lower-deck vestibules from new. The bodies were built in Aberdeen's own workshops on Brill 21E trucks. The trucks were later replaced by Peckham P35s. The batch was withdrawn between 1950 and 1953.

99

No 99 was delivered in 1923 as an experimental high-speed tram using an Aberdeen-built body on a Brill 21E truck; the latter was subsequently replaced by a Peckham P35. It survived in service until 1956.

Two batches of fully enclosed trams were delivered in 1924/25 (Nos 100-06) and 1926-31 (Nos 116-24) that were supplied with bodies built in Aberdeen's own workshops. The earlier cars were the first to have Peckham P35 trucks for service in Aberdeen. All the second batch, although not all initially supplied with P35s, eventually received them. No 102 is seen here at Woodside on 22 May 1955. Michael H. Waller

Between the two batches of fully enclosed trams supplied with corporation-built bodies, Aberdeen also received ten fully enclosed trams with Brush bodies, Nos 106-115. No 107 is pictured at the Bridge of Don terminus on 3 May 1958. The Brush-built trams were known as 'The English Cars', while the enclosed wooden-bodied cars were known as 'Standards'.
Michael H. Waller

100-105/116-124
These two batches were completed in 1924/25 (Nos 100-105) and 1926-31 (116-124) with bodies again built in the corporation's own workshops. Nos 100-105/120/123 were fitted with Peckham P35 trucks from new. Nos 116-119 were originally fitted with Brill 79E, Nos 121/122 with Brill 21E and 124 an EMB Hornless; all these were eventually fitted with P35 trucks. All were withdrawn from service between 1955 and 1958.

106-115
Supplied in 1925 with Brush bodies on Peckham P35 four-wheel trucks, this batch of ten was fully enclosed from new. The batch was withdrawn between 1953 and 1958.

126-137
This batch of 12 cars was supplied in 1929 with Brush fully enclosed bodies on Peckham P35 four-wheel trucks. Withdrawal occurred between 1955 and 1958.

Brush supplied a further batch of 12 fully enclosed trams to Aberdeen, Nos 126-137, in 1929. The last of the type is seen at Castle Street on 3 March 1951.
Michael H. Waller

One of the two streamlined centre-entrance bogie cars, No 139, awaits its next duty at Bridge of Don in 1947. The four cars were designed to be test beds for future orders but proved to be the last new trams built by English Electric. Michael H. Waller

138-141

Delivered in 1940, shortly after the outbreak of the Second World War, were four streamlined trams supplied with English Electric bodies. Two, Nos 138/39, were fitted with EMB Lightweight bogies, and the remaining two were fitted with EMB Hornless four-wheel trucks; the bogie cars could seat 74, ten more than the four-wheelers. In 1945, the cars were all fitted with a public address system to enable the stops to be announced; at this date the two bogie cars were largely used on the Bridges and Hazlehead routes, and the two four-wheelers operated on the latter. In 1954/55 the two bogie cars were modified with power-operated platform doors, with the seating increased by two to 76. The four cars were withdrawn between 1956 and 1958.

Alongside the two bogie streamlined cars, Aberdeen also took delivery of two four-wheel streamlined cars in 1940. The bogie cars could accommodate 74 seated passengers but the capacity of the four-wheel cars was only 64. One of the latter, No 141, is seen on St Nicholas Street in April 1951. Latterly allocated to the Woodside route, the two saw little use after the conversion of that route. Michael H. Waller

DUNDEE

Map of the Dundee network as at 1945.

The smallest of the four surviving Scottish tramways, Dundee possessed at the end of the Second World War a network of radiating lines – to Blackness, Downfield, Lochee, Maryfield and Ninewells – operated by some 60 four-wheel, fully enclosed trams.

Electric tramcars had started operating over the system on 13 July 1900 and by the outbreak of the First World War in 1914 the network was effectively complete. At its peak the system operated 99 trams but, during the interwar years, a number of routes were abandoned or converted to bus operation. The first to succumb was the short section to Craig Pier, which had never been successful; that was abandoned on 1 June 1919. The Constitution Road route, over which single-deck combination cars operated, was abandoned on 26 February 1928. The takeover of the Dundee, Broughty Ferry & District Co on 5 November 1930 resulted in the conversion of the route to Monifieth to bus operation. The track

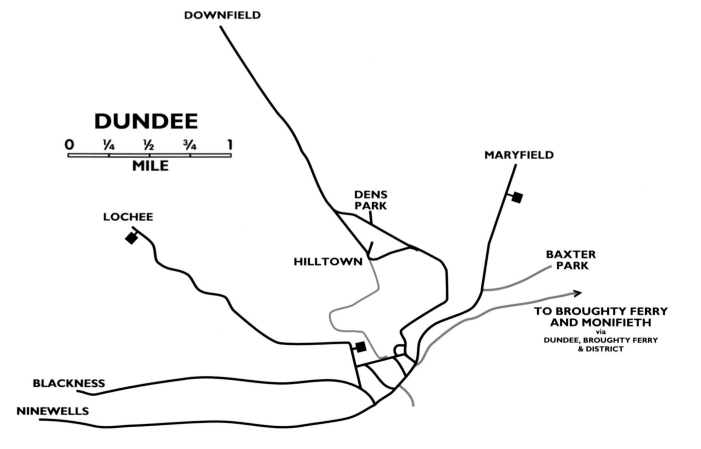

The most modern cars on the Dundee system were the ten 'Lochee' cars – Nos 19-28 – that were delivered in 1930. They were also wider than the rest of the fleet, which precluded them operating, other than on the Lochee route, more than one at a time as the track separation on the other routes was not great enough to permit them to pass safely. No 19 is seen here at Lochee on 25 January 1948. Michael H. Waller

as far as Belsize Road was corporation-owned; beyond there to the Monifieth terminus, it was company-owned. Finally, on 2 October 1932, the Baxter Park service was converted to bus operation and the route extended to serve a new housing estate. Not all was negative, however, as ten new trams – the wider 'Lochee' cars – were delivered in 1930 and many of the older cars were fully rebuilt as enclosed four-wheelers. In addition, a new central depot and workshop was completed in 1929 and, on 3 July 1933, the Lindsay Street link was opened in the city centre. Although there were proposals for further extensions, this proved to be the last new link opened in the city. In 1933 the first car was converted to operate using the Fischer bow collector; the bulk of the fleet was so equipped by the end of 1935.

Originally delivered as a balcony car in 1921, No 40 was rebuilt once and renumbered twice during its career in Dundee. It is seen here at the Ninewells terminus in May 1948. Michael H. Waller

On 29 August 1948, Dundee No 5, a car originally supplied in 1900 but much rebuilt during its life of more than 50 years, awaits departure from the terminus at Blackness with a service for Downfield.
Michael H. Waller

Dundee entered the post-war era with a pro-tram general manager in Robert Taylor, but he was conscious in early 1946 that, despite the role of trams on key routes into the city, the lack of long-term planning including 'development of the tramway routes' was impossible. Although there was no long-term plan, the authority was investing significant amounts in track relaying. In late 1947 some track in the centre was relaid, and in early 1948 the relaying of the Downfield route was completed along with one mile of the outward track on the Lochee route and both lines on the Step Row-Blackness Avenue section of the route to Ninewells. Further work later in 1948 included the loop in Albert Square, which resulted in revised working with the cars now entering from the north end and no longer running against the traffic flow, and the remainder of the High Street.

With the Clydesdale Bank on the corner, Dundee No 11 heads eastbound into High Street from Murraygate with a service from Downfield to Blackness on 30 August 1948.
Michael H. Waller

One of the four fully enclosed trams delivered in 1926, by now renumbered 32, is seen traversing the loop in Albert Square on 26 March 1949. The Gothic Revival building in the background was known as the Albert Institute and was built to a design of the noted Victorian architect Sir George Gilbert Scott between 1865 and 1867. Today, known as the McManus Galleries, it still houses the city's museum and art gallery.
Michael H. Waller

One of Dundee's problems was the age of the fleet. The newest cars were the ten 'Lochee' cars that were already 15 years old, and many of the other cars, although rebuilt, had their origins before the First World War. In late 1947 Taylor inspected Glasgow No 1005 and was impressed; the problem, however, was that the narrow separation between the inward and outward lines on all routes except that to Lochee prevented the operation of normal-width standard-gauge cars. The 'Lochee' cars were wider and could only operate on other routes singly to avoid

Dundee possesses two football clubs: Dundee United, based at Tannadice, and Dundee, based at Dens Park. The two grounds were located within a stone's throw of each other and football specials ran to home matches. A special siding was provided on Provost Road for the purpose and, on 25 March 1950, a line-up of cars, headed by No 49, await the returning fans. Michael H. Waller

Work in progress on the relaying of the track in Murraygate on 16 September 1950. This was to be the last significant trackwork undertaken in the city centre. Following closure, the track was left in situ and is still extant today – the most conspicuous reminder in the twenty-first century that Dundee once possessed a tramway system. Michael H. Waller

any possible collision on the narrow sections. This meant that Dundee was unable to take advantage of the disposal of more modern cars as they were withdrawn elsewhere.

In October 1947, Nos 57-60 were scrapped; these had not operated for a decade and had not been fitted with bow collectors. Any spare parts were retained. This reduced the fleet to 56, the number that remained operational until the final run-down of the system during 1955/56. The surviving cars underwent considerable maintenance; through to early 1949, a number of the cars – 34/36/37/39, 41-44/46-49 – were refurbished and repainted. On 9 November 1948 No 42 was slightly damaged in a derailment at the junction of Tay Street and Nethergate, but the tram was quickly repaired and returned to service.

As elsewhere, Dundee faced increasingly strained financial circumstances during the immediate post-war years and there were applications to raise or revise fares. The most notable occurred in late 1947 when the corporation sought to eliminate the ½d fare (Dundee was the last place in Britain to offer such a fare); this was approved and implemented in March 1948.

Despite the financial pressures there were no overt signs that the trams were under threat. During 1949, as supplies of new tram track became available again, the inbound section of Nethergate was relaid, and the 'Lochee' cars were overhauled and repainted. All bar ten of the tram fleet was so treated in the post-war years. On 12 December 1950 the Transport Committee met; it examined the possibility of adopting trolleybuses – Dundee had operated this type of

transport earlier (between 1912 and 1914) and Glasgow had just introduced them – as well as the subject of acquiring new trams. It was decided to form a sub-committee composed of the general manager plus convener of the committee (G. W. Davidson) to investigate. The *Scottish Daily Mail* of 14 March 1950 reported that Dundee Corporation was investigating the future of its tramway, although nothing as yet indicated that the system was under threat. Indeed, during the financial year ending on 31 May 1950, the trams made a profit of £7,800 as against a loss of £14,000 on the buses despite the lower fares charged on the trams. It was expected that in the year to 31 May 1951 the trams would make a profit of £22,945 against a loss of £47,000 on the buses.

Much of the activity over the next couple of years suggested that the trams had a future. Work continued on tram overhauls and improvement. No 51, for example, was fitted with a new motor and had its EMB truck modified during

the summer of 1950, No 52 received a new DK105 motor during the summer of 1952 and Nos 1-18 were passing through the works for overhaul. In terms of track, work continued; during the autumn of 1950 the important section through Murraygate was completely relaid. (This track still exists and forms one of the few tangible signs in Dundee that the city ever possessed a tramway system.) In early 1951 the tram livery was modified; the tradition of having the city's coat of arms at either end of the trams was abandoned in favour of advertising panels. In January 1952 it was reported that the Lord Provost commented that the number of buses using termini in the centre needed to be reduced and he advocated the use of continental-type trams with the buses providing feeder services. Later in the year it was rumoured that second-hand trams were to be acquired and that the extension to the Lochee route – first mooted in 1938 but shelved due to the war – was to be progressed. In late 1952 the Transport

In 1951 Dundee Corporation abandoned its policy of having the coat of arms at each end of its trams to accommodate advertising; No 26, seen here at Lochee on 2 August 1952, reflects this new policy. Michael H. Waller

Supplied as an
open-top bogie
car by ER&TCW in
1900, by 2 August
1952, when recorded
at the Downfield
terminus, No 9 was
already more than
50 years old; it was
the perceived age of
much of the tram
fleet that counted
against it when
Colonel Robert
McCreary came to
prepare his report on
the system's future.
Michael H. Waller

Committee decided on tramcar retention
and this was reflected in work carried out.
No 53 received a new motor, and much
track, including sections of the Lochee
and Downfield routes, was relaid. No 47,
seriously damaged in a collision with
a lorry, was repaired and returned to
service.

However, not all was positive. In March
1953 Colonel Robert McCreary, who had
retired as general manager of Belfast in
1951, produced a report that advocated
tramway conversion by the end of 1956,
citing the age of the tramcar fleet as
being unsustainable. On 26 April 1953,
those cars serving Downfield that had
been routed via Moncur Crescent were
routed via Hilltown, although the track
was retained for duplicate and football
traffic as required. The uncertainty was
reflected in a campaign in the local
media in favour of tramcar retention and,
certainly for a period, work continued
on tramcar improvement with Nos 54

and 55 receiving new DK305 motors
in late 1953; these were the first cars to
emerge in a new and much simplified
livery. Other work saw the replacement
of bracket arms in Perth Road by span
wires; this meant that the last surviving
bracket arms on the system were those on
North Tay Street. Also in late 1953 a sub-
committee was appointed under Bailie
William Hughes to investigate again the
possibility of acquiring new or second-
hand trams. In the spring of 1954 No 56
was remotored; this was the last car to be
so treated. On 3 May 1954, Nos 37 and 46
collided at the junction of Tay Street and
Nethergate; one passenger was injured
and both trams were damaged. Both were
restored to traffic.

Despite the overall good condition of
the system, its death knell was foretold
in a report prepared by the new general
manager, W. L. Russell, in late 1954.
In it he advocated complete tramway
conversion. The replacement of the fleet

To mark the Coronation of HM Queen Elizabeth II, Dundee Corporation ran No 1 suitably bedecked. It is seen here at the Maryfield terminus on 3 June 1953. Michael H. Waller

Dundee No 42, which dated originally to 1920 when it was delivered as No 68 (adopting the fleet number of one of Dundee's short-lived trolleybuses), is pictured at Maryfield on 26 June 1953. Michael H. Waller

One of the ten 'Lochee' cars, No 24, pictured in July 1955 after the adoption of advertising; one can't help feeling that this particular advert – given that the city was home to Keiller's Dundee marmalade – was perhaps a tad ill placed! W. G. S. Hyde/Online Transport Archive (1/17)

was overdue; he estimated the cost of acquiring 56 new trams at £532,000 as against £247,500 to acquire the requisite number of replacement buses; track repairs and modification was costed at £76,854 for the first year and £26,396 annually thereafter. This policy was vociferously opposed in the local press and by certain councillors. Despite the opposition of a number of the latter, a plan for the experimental conversion of the route from Blackness to Downfield was approved in early January 1955. The opposition was based on the fact that,

once implemented, the policy would be very difficult to reverse (as indeed proved to be the case).

Despite the threat to the tramway system, work continued on routine maintenance. The 'Lochee' cars were overhauled and repainted in spring 1955, and the single-track section between Hyndland Street and West Park Road was relaid. Elsewhere, however, the state of the track, most notably on the threatened Blackness section, was increasingly poor and a number of trams looked careworn. As a result of the delay in obtaining replacement buses, trams continued to operate the Blackness-Downfield route until 27 November 1955 when the route was converted to bus operation. As a result, 25 cars – Nos 1-18, 29, 51-56 – were advertised for sale.

Following the conversion, Russell reported in February 1956 on plans for the conversion of the remainder of the system, using 30 second-hand buses acquired from London Transport at £1,750 each. This plan was approved by a vote of 8-2 in the Transport Committee on 27 June 1956 and by a vote of the full council of 24-9 two months later. The decision to make the Blackness-Downfield conversion permanent was made by the council on 5 July 1956; the fact that the 25 withdrawn trams had been scrapped, although the track and overhead had been retained, made the decision inevitable. In September 1956 it was announced that the final conversion would take place on 20 October 1956, three weeks earlier than originally anticipated. The system closed with no official ceremony as services were withdrawn from the two remaining routes; the final service was a convoy of six cars that departed from Maryfield for Lochee Road with No 25 bringing up the rear as the final car in service. This was not quite to be the end as, between 20 October and 25 October, the surviving

On 26 November 1955, No 4 is seen on Brook Street with a service to Blackness. This was to be the last day of the Blackness-Downfield service before its proposed suspension for 12 months; in reality the trams never returned. No 4 was one of the trams withdrawn for scrap following the conversion.
Michael H. Waller

cars were moved to Maryfield depot for scrapping; the last car that made this trip was 'Lochee' car No 21.

With Dundee's demise, the last tramway in Britain with significant single-track sections and passing loops, passed into history. Unfortunately, although two cars – a 'Lochee' car and one of the two single-deck works cars – were offered for preservation, the lack of suitable storage in an age before the Tramway Museum Society had acquired the site at Crich meant that the offer had to be declined. It was estimated in 1956 that the cost of

The last day of trams in Dundee – 20 October 1956 – and three trams, with 'Lochee' car No 28 closest to the camera, are seen at the terminus of the Lochee route.
Michael H. Waller

road reinstatement would be £480,000; in reality the cost of tramway conversion proved significantly higher than forecast. In January 1960 the City Engineer reported that the total cost of road repairs resulting from the conversion programme was £750,000.

Dundee Depots

Dundee possessed two small tram depots for its fleet: Lochee, located just south of the terminus, and Maryfield, again sited just south of the terminus. Both were closed to trams with the final abandonment of the system on 20 October 1956; Maryfield depot was used after then for the scrapping of the remaining fleet). In addition to the two operational depots, the corporation also possessed workshops located closer to the city centre at the corner of Lochee Road and Dudhope Road. Until 1921 this had also been an operational depot but was refurbished in 1929 to become the main workshops. It continued to handle tram maintenance until final closure on 20 October 1956.

Dundee Closures

26 November 1955	Blackness-Downfield
20 October 1956	Maryfield-Ninewells/ City-Lochee

Dundee Fleet
1-10

Dating from 1900, Nos 1-10 were the first electric tramcars delivered to Dundee. When new, they were supplied by ER&TCW with open-top and open-vestibule bodies on Brill 22E bogies. Top covers were fitted to the batch between 1907 and 1910 and all ten were completely rebuilt as fully enclosed four-wheelers on EMB flexible trucks in 1930/31. All 10 were withdrawn from service in 1955 following the suspension of the Blackness-Downfield service.

When delivered, Dundee's first electric trams were open-top bogie cars; by the end of their careers, however, they had all been converted to fully enclosed four-wheelers. No 8 is pictured here at the Blackness terminus on 6 April 1952. Michael H. Waller

When delivered, Dundee's first electric trams were open-top bogie cars; by the end of their careers, however, they had all been converted to fully enclosed four-wheelers. No 8 is pictured here at the Blackness terminus on 6 April 1952. Michael H. Waller

With track repair work being undertaken in the foreground, No 13 is seen on Strathmartin Road, on the Downfield route, on 12 April 1952. Like Nos 1-10, Nos 11-18 were originally built as open-top bogie cars and converted to fully enclosed four-wheelers in the 1930s. Michael H. Waller

11-18

Originally numbered 41-8 and delivered in 1902, Nos 11-18 were built as open-top unvestibuled cars. Fitted with Milnes-built bodies, the cars were fitted with Brill 22E bogies when new. The trams were fitted with top covers in 1906/07 with Nos 44-46 receiving replacement Hurst Nelson top covers in 1916 and the remainder in 1925.

Renumbered Nos 11-18 in 1927, the batch was rebuilt as fully enclosed four-wheelers in 1928-30 and fitted with EMB 79EX four-wheel trucks (although Nos 11 and 12 had been fitted earlier with Peckham P35 trucks). All were withdrawn in 1955, again following the suspension of the service between Blackness and Downfield.

Pictured on 16 August 1950 at Downfield, with the sidings serving the ex-LMS line from Dundee to Newtyle station forming a backdrop, 'Lochee' No 27 was being used for an LRTL tour. Width restrictions prevented the 'Lochee' cars from operating all but the route from the city centre to Lochee usually, although single cars could traverse the other four remaining routes.
Michael H. Waller

19-28

The last wholly new trams delivered to Dundee, the ten 'Lochee' cars were supplied with Brush fully enclosed bodies on EMB Flexible axle four-wheel trucks. Wider than the earlier trams, they were restricted to operation mainly on the route to Lochee, where the track separation was normal, although they could traverse the other routes provided they were not scheduled to pass. All ten of the batch survived until the system's final closure in October 1956 with No 25 being the last tram in service.

Although one of the batch was offered for preservation, this proved impractical and all were scrapped.

29-33

This quintet of trams was built in 1925 (No 29) and 1926 (Nos 30-33) and had originally been numbered 95-99 when new. Fully enclosed from new, the trams were fitted with bodies built in Dundee's own workshops on Peckham P35 four-wheel trucks. The trams were renumbered Nos 81-85 in 1928 and to 29-33 in 1936. All were withdrawn in 1956.

Originally numbered 97 when built in 1926, No 31 was renumbered 83 in 1928, becoming No 31 eight years later. It was one of nine trams built between 1923 and 1926 that had fully enclosed bodies built in the corporation's own workshops. No 31 is recorded here at Ninewells on 27 August 1948.
Michael H. Waller

34-51

These 18 trams were all supplied with Hurst Nelson bodies on Brill 21E trucks in 1916 (Nos 47-50), 1920 (Nos 41-6) and 1921 (34-40, 51) and were originally numbered 75-78, 67/68, 79-82 and 83-90 respectively. The cars were originally open-balcony and vestibuled, but were rebuilt as fully enclosed in 1932-33 when they were fitted with EMB Flexible axle four-wheel trucks, with the exception of No 90 (51 after 1936) that was fitted with an EMB Swing axle truck. Nos 77/78 were renumbered 73/74 in 1927 and the resulting Nos 73-76 became Nos 47-50 in 1936. Nos 79-82 were renumbered 43-46 in 1928. Nos 83-90 became Nos 47-54 in 1928 and then Nos 34-40, 51 in 1936. All were withdrawn in 1956 with the exception of No 51 that succumbed the previous year.

Two of the Hurst Nelson-bodied cars delivered between 1916 and 1921 pass on Perth Road at its junction with West Park Road on 3 June 1953. No 38 of 1921 was originally built as No 87, becoming No 51 in 1927 and No 38 in 1936. No 48 was built as No 78 in 1916, becoming No 74 in 1927 and No 48 nine years later. Michael H. Waller

One of the three cars to survive the Second World War from the batch built by Milnes Voss in 1908, No 59 – seen here outside Maryfield Depot on 9 April 1939 – had originally been No 63. F. K. Farrell Collection/Online Transport Archive

No 56 was one of a quartet of trams built between 1923 and 1925 that were Dundee's first trams to be built as fully enclosed from new. Fitted with bodies built in the corporation's workshops, the four were originally fitted with Brill 21E trucks but these were replaced and by 1947, the date of this photograph taken in Albert Square, all were operating on EMB Flexible trucks. *Michael H. Waller*

52, 58/59

These were the post-war survivors of a batch of six cars, Nos 61-66, delivered in 1908 that were built with Milnes Voss open-balcony bodies on Brill 21E trucks. No 61 was rebuilt as a fully enclosed car on an EMB Hornless four-wheel truck in 1933 and renumbered 52 in 1936. Nos 62/63 were renumbered 58/59 in 1936 and retained their original open-balcony bodies on Brill 21E trucks until withdrawal in 1947; they survived post-war for use on football specials. No 52 was withdrawn in 1952.

53-56

This quartet of trams was delivered between 1923 and 1925 as Nos 91-94; they were fitted from new with fully enclosed bodies built in the corporation's workshops on Brill 21E trucks. Renumbered Nos 77-80 in 1928, all four were fitted with EMB Flexible trucks in 1930. These were replaced again by EMB Hornless trucks in 1933 and the trams renumbered to 53-56 in 1936. The four were withdrawn in 1955, again as a result of the suspension of the service from Blackness to Downfield.

57/60

These two cars were the last survivors of a batch of six, Nos 55-60, that was new in 1907. Fitted with Brush open-balcony bodies and Brill 21E trucks, the cars remained un-rebuilt through their careers, being withdrawn in 1947. No 57 had originally been numbered 55, being renumbered 56 in 1936.

RW1/RW2

These two single-deck works cars were, like Nos 57 and 60, part of the batch of six trams delivered in 1907. Originally numbered 56 and 57, the two were converted for works purposes in 1935. The duo survived until the closure of the system in 1956; one was again made available for preservation but this was also unsuccessful.

One of the single-deck repair cars, cut down from passenger cars in 1935, No 2 is recorded outside Maryfield depot on 16 August 1950. Michael H. Waller

EDINBURGH

Map of the
Edinburgh network
as at 1945.

The city of Edinburgh was a relatively late recruit to the operators of electric tramcars, as much of the system inherited by the corporation from Edinburgh & District Co on 30 June 1919 was cable-operated and the first electric trams, on the section from Ardmillan Terrace to Slateford, had commenced operation as late as 8 June 1910. The corporation's electric network expanded on 20 November 1920 when Leith Corporation

was incorporated. The conversion of the cable tramways commenced on 20 June 1922 with the inauguration of electric trams on the Leith via the Grange to Nether Liberton and Churchill. The conversion programme took a year, with the last route – that to Portobello – being converted on 23 June 1923.

Between the withdrawal of the final cable cars and the outbreak of the Second World War, Edinburgh was one of the more progressive of British tramways,

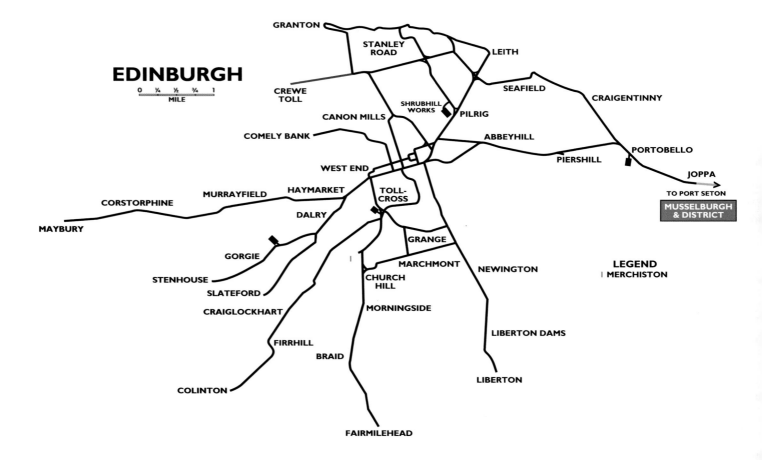

A view of the terminus at Corstorphine with cars on routes 1 and 12; the section illustrated here was the last extension completed in Edinburgh. Although work commenced on the route to Crewe Toll, this was never completed. The appearance of two older cars on routes 1 and 12 was unusual as, post-war, these routes were generally operated by more modern trams. F. N. T. Lloyd-Jones/ Online Transport Archive

building extensions – the last being the extension of the Corstorphine route to Maybury opened on 14 February 1937 – and constructing a significant number of new trams during the period. Further extensions were authorised and work authorised on the construction of the route to Crewe Toll on 6 January 1938. Actual construction, however, was delayed until 1939 and then suspended once war broke out.

At its peak, Edinburgh operated a fleet of some 400 trams over a network of just over 47 route miles. In 1945, with the

No 141 heads east along Inverleith Gardens, having just turned from Granton Road, with a service for Colinton. The junction in the foreground represented the point at which the proposed route to Crewe Toll would have taken; in reality, this route was never completed and the junction remained unused. F. N. T. Lloyd-Jones/ Online Transport Archive

Edinburgh No 161, new in 1931, stands at the city centre terminus of route 21, in front of the General Post Office on Waterloo Place, awaiting its next duty towards Levenhall on 25 June 1949.
Michael H. Waller

return of peace, Edinburgh was widely regarded as one of the most secure of Britain's tramways. The pre-war policy of constructing replacement trams continued, with the first post-war car – No 51 – emerging in 1945. In all, 18 new trams were built between then and 1950. That the tram was seen as having a future was demonstrated in early 1945 when the Public Utilities Committee voted to recommence work on the Granton-Crewe Toll extension at a cost of £24,000 with work having been 25 per cent completed

before the wartime suspension. There were, however, straws in the wind that suggested that the tram network was not wholly secure; in the spring of 1946, for example, the Edinburgh Accident Prevention Committee produced a fourteen-point plan to improve road safety. One of the committee's proposals was for the conversion of the tram services to bus operation. More positive was the purchase, in late 1946, of 11 of the withdrawn 'Pilcher' cars at £210 from Manchester Corporation.

On 25 June 1949 No 280 is seen at the bottom of The Mound with a service bound for Granton Road station.
Michael H. Waller

On 23 August 1950, Edinburgh No 215 stands at the Fairmilehead terminus of route No 16 with a service for Granton. Michael H. Waller

Perhaps the critical point in the story of Edinburgh's trams post-war was the death, in September 1948 while on holiday, of the general manager, Robert McLeod, who had held the role since 2 May 1935. He was succeeded by his deputy, William Morrison Little, who had left Edinburgh in 1941 to take the position as general manager of St Helens and then Reading (both trolleybus operators)

before returning to Edinburgh in 1946. McLeod was a tram man; Little was perhaps more equivocal when faced by the undertaking's deteriorating financial position. The annual report for the year to 25 May 1949 recorded losses on both the tram and bus operations.

On 17 October 1949 routes 7, 11 and 28 were extended from Stanley Road to Craighall Road. This was over track that

Edinburgh No 219 is pictured at Tollcross on 23 July 1951 with a service to Stanley Road. Michael H. Waller

In August 1950 No 275, one of the cars built by Leeds Forge in 1923, is seen at Comely Bank. The relatively short but heavily-used route 24 from Comely Bank to Waverley station was converted to bus operation on 1 June 1952. This was the first conversion that resulted in track abandonment.
R. W. A. Jones/Online Transport Archive (EH12)

had not been in regular passenger use for some 30 years and required overhead from the crossover at the new terminus and the removal of the trolley reverser at the old. Although this was positive, Little recommended the conversion of the loss-making route 18 – Liberton Dams to Waverley via Newington, Toll Cross and the West End. This was effected on 26 March 1950; there was no track abandoned at this stage, and the five cars used on the route were redeployed to other services. Withdrawn at this time, but partially balanced by the construction of a new No 48, were the last two of the 1922-type cars: No 125 after sustaining damage in a collision and No 136.

That the tramway in Edinburgh was now under serious threat became evident in June 1950 when Little produced a report advocating conversion of 25 per cent of the system to bus operation over a five-year period. This proposal inevitably caused much local debate, mostly hostile

to the idea of tramway conversion. However, the Transport Committee, led by its convenor Councillor Harkess, voted to accept the plan, although the full council initially rejected the proposal. In September 1950 the Transport Committee again supported the plan and, on 2 November 1950, the full council voted 41-17 to implement it. Opposition remained strong, and a detailed conversion plan was not produced until the next autumn; in the meantime a certain amount of trackwork was undertaken. This included the removal of the facing junction at Waterloo Place, which had never been used regularly. Another casualty was the junction for the proposed route to Crewe Toll; with partial closure now planned the cost of completing the project – never restarted after the Second World War – could not be justified. Following the abandonment of the project, the overhead was removed in March 1951 and the partially laid track in

October 1953. On 18 September 1951 the *Edinburgh Evening Post* reported that the first routes to be converted were those to Comely Bank, Stenhouse and Slateford; these plans were formally approved by the council on 27 September 1951.

The closure process commenced on 1 June 1952 when buses replaced trams on route 24 from Waverley to Comely Bank; the next routes proposed for closure were the 2, 3 and 4. It was announced in the summer that when route 2 (and the Saturday afternoon relief on route 22 between Leith and Robertson Avenue/ Stenhouse) was converted, that track in George Street would be abandoned; this was a threat to the flexibility of the tramways as George Street provided the only diversionary route in the event of Princes Street being blocked or closed. The belief that the 25 per cent plan would foreshadow abandonment was confirmed on 15 July 1952 when complete conversion was announced; the policy

was confirmed by a vote of 31-21 by the full council on 25 September 1952. The policy was to be completed over a three-year period; the change of policy came, it was alleged, by the requirements of the Ministry of Transport for tramway retention for at least 20 years to justify a major loan to fund track repairs.

On 24 August 1952 route 25 was extended from Drum Brae to Corstorphine, and route 26 was curtailed from Drum Brae to the Zoo. This was followed on 14 December 1952 by the conversion of route 2, Stenhouse to Granton via George Street, to bus operation. Between the end of the war and the end of 1952 some 26 trams had been withdrawn; these included Nos 121-136, the original electric cars, as well as Nos 36, 143, 241/44/45/46/49/55 and 324/49. These had succumbed due to either accidental damage or defect and had all been scrapped at Shrubhill. A further 60 trams were now offered for

Edinburgh No 148, built at Shrubhill in 1934, is pictured at Saughton Bridge; route 2, between Stenhouse and Graton via Leith, was converted to bus operation on 14 December 1952. R. W. A. Jones/Online Transport Archive (EH44)

sale as scrap; these were bought by James N. Connell Ltd of Coatbridge at £87 each. The condemned cars were driven under their own power to the Corstophine terminus where they were loaded onto Connell's lorry for onward shipment. The first two cars to suffer this fate were Nos 270 and 340 on 16 March 1953. Before despatch, the transport department transferred Maley & Taunton trucks to the withdrawn cars to ensure the surviving cars were fitted with Peckham trucks.

The next phase of the conversion programme took effect on 28 March 1953 with the conversion of route 3, Stenhouse to Newington. The track to Gorgie depot, however, remained in use until after the conversion of route 4 on 3 May 1953 when the trams to operate route 1 were transferred from Gorgie to Tollcross depot. A further indication of the decline in the tram system came with the removal of the passenger islands before a royal visit in June 1953. The conversion of route 4, Slateford to Piershill, occurred on 3 May 1953; this was the last phase of the original plan to scrap 25 per cent of the system. The estimated cost of lifting the track and reinstating the road on the

Comely Bank, Stenhouse and Slateford sections as well as along George Street was £83,000 with £27,000 recovered from the scrap released.

On 31 January 1954 there were several controversial service alterations. Route 10 was altered to run via Foot of Leith Walk and Ferry Road in place of route 16, which was rerouted to run via Bernard Street and became a part-day service. Route 27 became a part-day service, with no operation after 7 pm on Sundays. Route 15 was curtailed to terminate at Braids, and route 28 was abandoned; these changes led to objections from the residents of Fairmilehead and were reversed on 10 May 1954. The next conversion occurred on 28 March 1954 with route 1, Corstorphine to Liberton, succumbing. Proposals to convert the route to Levenhall were deferred due to objections to the corporation's proposed replacement bus services by SMT. On 6 June 1954 route 27 was curtailed from Firhill to Craiglockhart station; this was again reversed, however, on 17 October 1954. This period saw the last of the ex-Manchester 'Pilcher' cars withdrawn.

On 21 December 1952 Edinburgh No 302 stands at the Stenhouse terminus of route 3 to Newington; this service was converted to bus operation three months later. Michael H. Waller

Route 12 between Joppa and Corstorphine was one of three routes converted to bus operation on 11 July 1954. Here Edinburgh No 209 stands at the Joppa terminus. The section beyond Joppa to Levenhall had originally been owned by Musselburgh & District and had been acquired by the corporation on 7 May 1931, having previously been operated by the corporation following the company's cessation of services in 1928. R. W. A. Jones/Online Transport Archive (EH17)

11 July 1954 saw the conversion of routes 12, 25 and 26 – Corstorphine/Zoo to Joppa, Portobello and Piershill respectively. This resulted in the cessation of the movement of withdrawn cars for scrap to the terminus, although the steady procession continued for a week after the actual closure until work commenced on the route's dismantling; the scrap merchant now collected the condemned cars from North Junction Street. These conversions were followed by the replacement of route 15 – Fairmilehead to King's Road via London Road – by buses on 19 September 1954 and by route 5 – Morningside station to Piershill via London Road – on 31 October 1954. The deferred abandonment of the routes

Route 5 from Piershill to Morningside was converted to bus operation on 31 October 1954; here one of 46 replacement cars built between 1934 and 1937, No 111, stands at the Piershill terminus. This was situated as a short stub off Piersfield Terrace; trams continued over Piersfield Terrace and Moira Terrace for a further month, until the conversion of routes 20 and 21. R. W. A. Jones/Online Transport Archive (EH1)

Services over route 21 to Levenhall were finally withdrawn on 14 November 1954; on 15 August 1950, ex-Manchester No 411 stands at the Levenhall terminus with a service for the General Post Office. Until 1928 the metals of Musselburgh & District extended a further six miles to Port Seton from this point. Michael H. Waller

from Waterloo Place to Musselburgh / Levenhall – routes 20 and 21 – took place on 13 November 1954 following agreement with SMT of the operation of buses outside the city's boundaries. The last tram to Levenhall was No 292, and the last car to Portobello depot was

No 291, which had been hired by the Portobello Masonic Lodge. Following the conversion, Portobello depot was closed to trams, although it stored withdrawn cars for a period.

At the start of 1955 15 tram services remained operational. However, the

One of the post-war cars, No 210, which was built in 1947, stands at the crossover in Granton Road awaiting departure with a service on route 8 for Newington station via Broughton Street. This service was converted to bus operation on 3 April 1955. Phil Tatt/Online Transport Archive (266)

When the Colinton route was completed in 1926 it included a short section of single track at Inchdrewer House; 1939-built No 239 is seen heading west over this short section as it heads towards Colinton on route 10. This service was converted to bus operation on 23 October 1955. Phil Tatt/Online Transport Archive (1222)

purchase of 100 new buses for delivery in 1956 to permit the final withdrawals was approved on 29 March 1955 and the first of four routes to be converted in 1955 – route 8, Granton to Newington station via Broughton Street – was replaced by buses on 3 April 1955. This was followed on 7 August 1955 by the conversion of route 27 – Granton Road station to Craiglockhart – and on 23 October 1955 by routes 9 and 10: Colinton to Granton and Leith respectively. There were now no trams serving Colinton or the Broughton Street to Canonmills section. Routes 7 and 17 were also planned for closure in late 1955 but survived for a further four months.

In March 1956, largely because of the poor state of the tram track on Princes Street, eastbound non-tram traffic was subject to a temporary diversion with an increased frequency of cars on route No 6 to compensate for the lack of buses. Also from 1 March 1956 route 16 was diverted to run via Leith Street rather than York Place. On 11 March, the delayed

On 7 March 1956, route 7 from Stanley Road to Liberton was converted to bus operation; here, 1935-built No 15 awaits departure from the Liberton terminus. Phil Tatt/Online Transport Archive (1217)

Edinburgh Nos 248 and 366 pass on Bernard Street on route 17; this route, which linked Granton and Newington station via Bernard Street, was converted to bus operation on 11 March 1956. R. W. A. Jones/Online Transport Archive (EH61)

Edinburgh No 150 is pictured on Melville Drive while operating on route 6 – the Marchmont Circle – which was this car's usual haunt. Fitted with non-standard turntable seats, No 150 was rarely seen on any other route. The 6 was converted to bus operation on 27 May 1956. Phil Tatt/Online Transport Archive (1208)

conversion of route 7 – Stanley Road to Liberton – and the abandonment of route 17 – Granton to Newington station via Bernard Street – took place. Following the withdrawal of the 17, a peak-hours service from the Post Office to Granton via Bernard Street was operated but without a route number due to complaints; this, along with routes 13 and 14, was operated from Leith depot. As if to demonstrate that the trams were soon to disappear, on 26 March 1956 No 32 ran over a bomb and was damaged, but there were no casualties.

The Edinburgh system was now into its last six months of operation. On 5 May 1956 Leith depot closed to trams with its allocation for routes 13 and 14 transferred temporarily to Shrubhill; the cars for these routes were transferred to Tollcross on 27 May 1956 when routes 6 – Marchmont Circle – and 19 – Tollcross to Craigentinny

In August 1955 Edinburgh No 23 makes its way at the top end of Leith Walk on route 19 heading southbound towards Tollcross. In the distance a car can be seen on route 9 towards Colinton. R. W. A. Jones/Online Transport Archive (EH81)

– were converted to bus operation. On 1 June 1956 the remaining trams serving Princes Street – routes 11, 13, 14 and 28 – were diverted to share York Place with the 16; this permitted the track and overhead between St Andrew Street and the Post Office to be removed and the temporary diversion of eastbound non-tram traffic to be cancelled. Such was the decline in the tram fleet that modern cars, such as Nos 11-30 and 231/39/40, were being withdrawn for scrap. Withdrawals at this time also included the railgrinder car.

The next conversion occurred on 16 June 1956 with the demise of routes 13 and 14 – the Granton and Churchill Circle – at which time the 16 was extended from Bernard Street to Granton. This extension, however, was shortlived as the next two conversions – routes 11 (Stanley Road/ Granton to Braids) and 16 (Stanley Road/ Granton to Fairmilehead) – took place on 12 September 1956.

By now the system had been reduced to two routes – the 23 and the 28 (Granton Road station to Morningside and Stanley

With the coal yard, harbour and Firth of Forth in the background, 1933-built No 239 rounds the curve at Granton Square while operating on route 14 – the Churchill Circle – which was converted to bus operation on 17 June 1956. Phil Tatt/Online Transport Archive (1239)

In August 1955 Edinburgh No 195 heads alongside Morningside Road having just departed from the terminal stub, the tracks seen heading to the left on Belhaven Terrace that served Morningside Road station, with a northbound service heading towards the city centre. The tracks in the foreground were used by routes to Braids and Fairmilehead at this time. R. W. A. Jones/Online Transport Archive (EN66)

Road to Braids respectively) – with some 40 cars operational. It was announced on 23 October that these two routes would be converted on 16 November; despite the Suez Crisis, which resulted in conversions elsewhere being postponed, there was to be no last-minute reprieve for Edinburgh's trams. By this date only some five trams were working on Sundays as only one route, the 23, operated with the 28 being a weekday peak service only. On 16 November the peak-hour route 23 ceased to operate at 7 pm. The final journeys on route 28 occurred at 7.40 pm with No 88 being the last car to depart from Braids towards Shrubhill; it was preceded by nine extra cars and No 172, which had been painted in a special white livery to mark the closure. As the convoy passed Morningside, it was joined by No 217 with the official party, and which became the official last tram. Following closure,

one of the post-war cars, No 35, was preserved; it is now part of the collection on display at the National Tramway Museum.

Edinburgh No 152 approaches the terminus at Craighall Road, Newhaven, with a route 28 service; routes 7, 11 and 28 had been relocated to this terminus from Stanley Road in 1949. Phil Tatt/Online Transport Archive (1227)

Edinburgh Depots

Shrubhill, Edinburgh's main workshops, where many trams were built and where a transport museum existed for some years with No 35 on display, was located on Leith Walk. It was also used as a running depot and survived until the system's closure on 16 November 1956. Other depots serving the Edinburgh system post-1945 were: Gorgie, situated to the west of Gorgie Road on the route to Stenhouse, survived until 2 May 1953 with the conversion of route 4; Portobello, situated at the extreme east of the system close to the terminus at Joppa, lost its tram allocation on 14 November 1954 with the conversion of the General Post Office-Joppa/Levenhall routes; Leith, located on Leith Walk slightly to the north-east of Shrubhill Works, closed on 5 May 1956; when the depot closed, there was no means of evacuating the remaining trams as a result of earlier track and overhead removal, so the final cars had to be towed away via Regent Street by lorry. Tollcross, served by a loop at Tollcross, closed with the system on 16 November 1956.

Edinburgh Closures

26 March 1950	18 – Liberton-Waverley
1 June 1952	24 – Waverley-Comely Bank
14 December 1952	2 – Stenhouse-Granton (via Leith);
	22 – Leith-Robertson Avenue/Stenhouse (Saturday afternoon relief)
29 March 1953	3 – Stenhouse-Newington
3 May 1953	4 – Piershill-Slateford
28 March 1954	1 – Corstorphine-Liberton
11 July 1954	12 – Corstorphine/Zoo Park-Joppa;
	25 – Corstorphine/Zoo Park-Portobello;
	26 – Corstorphine/Zoo Park-Piershill
19 September 1954	15 – Fairmilehead-Portobello (Kings Road)
31 October 1954	5 – Piershill -Morningside
14 November 1954	21 – General Post Office-Levenhall

The depot at Leith was accessed from Leith Walk as shown here by ex-Manchester No 409 emerging from the depot and heading towards the north. R. W. A. Jones/Online Transport Archive (EH57)

3 April 1955	8 – Granton-Newington station (via Broughton Street)
7 August 1955	27 – Granton Road station-Craiglockhart (via The Mound)
23 October 1955	9 – Colinton-Granton;
	10 – Colinton-Leith
11 March 1956	17 – Granton-Newington station (via Bernard Street)
27 May 1956	6 – Marchmont Circle;
	19 – Tollcross-Craigentinny
17 June 1956	13/14 – Granton and Churchill Circle
12 September 1956	11 – Stanley Road/Granton-Braids;
	16 – Stanley Road/Granton-Fairmilehead
16 November 1956	23 – Granton Road station-Morningside;
	28 – Stanley Road-Braids

Edinburgh Fleet
11-18

Although Hurst Nelson supplied the parts, the steel bodies for this batch of eight trams delivered in 1935 were completed at Shrubhill Works on Peckham P22 trucks; Nos 11/12/16 operated with M&T Swing link trucks between 1948 and 1953. All eight were withdrawn in 1956.

19-24

With steel bodies supplied by English Electric on Peckham P22 trucks, this batch of six cars entered service in 1935. Nos 21-24 later operated on EMB hornless trucks. All survived until withdrawal in 1956.

One of the six cars delivered in 1935 from English Electric with steel bodywork and sloping ends, No 24 is seen at the Colinton terminus of route 10. Approaching in the distance is No 238, one of the 46 replacement cars delivered between 1934 and 1937 that followed on from No 69. No 238 was constructed in 1937. J. Joyce/Online Transport Archive (JT72)

Edinburgh No 26 was one of a batch of six replacement steel-bodied cars supplied by Metropolitan-Cammell of Birmingham in 1935. No 26 is seen crossing the Bernard Street swing bridge on route 17 from Newington station to Granton. By the date of the photograph the entire batch had been retrucked with Peckham P22 trucks. All were withdrawn for scrap in 1956. R. W. A. Jones/Online Transport Archive (EH62)

25-30
Also delivered in 1935 was this batch of six trams fitted with Metropolitan-Cammell steel bodies on M&T Swing link trucks. All six were retrucked to Peckham P22s in about 1953 and survived in service until 1956.

31/33/34/36/38, 42-44/46, 53/57/58, 60/61/64/65/68, 70/74/75/77-81/84-86/89, 94, 100/01/04/06/07/09/13-19/38-44/46-49/51-56/58/59/61-63/66-68/74-79/81-85/87/88/91-94/96-98, 200/01/03/05-08/64/68
From the mid-1920s Edinburgh started to replace the converted cable cars on a like-for-like basis, with new electric cars known as 'Wooden Standards' taking the number of the cable car they replaced and often reusing the top deck from the older vehicles. The first of these cars appeared in 1924 and production continued through to 1934 with No 191. Nos 61, 75/78, 84/86 and 138/51/82/84 were renumbered in 1935 from 16, 3, 24, 6, 7, 29, 28, 18 and 20 respectively. All were built with bodies supplied by Shrubhill Works on Peckham P22 trucks. Nos 177 and 264, both delivered in 1932, were fitted with EMB trucks during 1932 and 1933, and 264 was later fitted with an M&T Swing link truck. All were withdrawn between 1950 and 1956.

From the mid-1920s Edinburgh undertook the replacement of the ex-cable cars through the construction of new electric cars, known as 'Wooden Standards', that took the numbers of the withdrawn cars they replaced. No 89, seen here at The Mound, was one of the last to be completed, entering service in 1933. No 89 survived until withdrawal in 1955. R. W. A. Jones/ Online Transport Archive (EH54)

No 47, seen here at Liberton, was one of the domed-roof fully enclosed cars built at Shrubhill between 1938 and 1950. In total 18 of the type were built post-war, including No 47 that dated to 1947, representing the last wholly new trams delivered for service with the corporation.
J. Joyce/Online Transport Archive (JT73)

32/35/37/39-41/45/47-52/54-56/59, 62/63/66/67/69, 71-73/76, 82/83/88, 91, 103/05/11/12/20/37/45/50/57/60/64/65/69, 172/73/89/90/95/99, 202/04/09/10-30/32-38/43/47/48/69

Based upon the experimental No 180, these trams, known as 'Domed Roof Standards', represented further replacement vehicles for withdrawn cable cars and took over the number of the earlier car that they replaced. The first of these fully enclosed domed-roof cars was No 69, built in 1934, with the last being No 225 in August 1950; this was the last new tram supplied to Edinburgh. All were built with bodies supplied by Shrubhill Works on underframes supplied by Hurst Nelson and were fitted with Peckham P22 trucks. All were withdrawn between 1954 and 1956 with No 172 being repainted in a special white livery to mark the system's closure in November 1956. No 35 was preserved following closure; for many years this was displayed at Shrubhill Works but is now at the National Tramway Museum.

In 1922 Edinburgh acquired a batch of 16 cars, Nos 121-36, from the local manufacturer McHardy & Elliot – the only trams that the company built for the corporation. Originally delivered with open balconies, all 16 were fully enclosed between 1930 and 1933. No 134 was the last of the type in service, surviving until withdrawal in 1952. Barry Cross Collection/Online Transport Archive

121-36

Supplied by McHardy & Elliot, but with upper-deck bodies built by Hurst Nelson, on Peckham P22 trucks, this batch of open-balcony cars was supplied in 1922. All were fully enclosed between 1930 and 1933. Withdrawal took place between 1949 and 1952.

180

This was an experimental straight-sided car built in Shrubhill Works on an ELB flexible axle four-wheel truck in 1932, reused from No 177; the truck was replaced by an M&T Swing link truck from No 264 later in 1932. From new until 1935 it operated in a bright red livery. No 180 survived until withdrawal in 1956.

No 180, seen here in Leith Walk, was the first of Edinburgh's experimental modern cars. Built at Shrubhill with a fully enclosed alloy frame body, the car was initially fitted with an EMB Swing-link truck, but this was soon replaced by a Maley & Taunton version. When new, the car operated in a bright red livery, which it retained until 1935. With its striking red livery when new, this car was known as 'Red Biddy'. R. W. A. Jones/Online Transport Archive (EH56)

One of the three Hurst Nelson-built cars from 1934, No 231, is pictured rounding the Granton Road curve; by the date of this photograph the car had had its original Swing-link truck replaced by a Peckham P22. R. W. A. Jones/ Online Transport Archive (EH49)

No 249, seen here at the Fairmilehead terminus of route 11, was one of six cars delivered in 1934 that were built with Metropolitan-Cammell steel bodies on M&T Swing-link trucks. No 249 was withdrawn in 1952. F. N. T. Lloyd-Jones/ Online Transport Archive

231/39/40

This trio of cars from 1934 was built with steel domed-roof bodies supplied by Hurst Nelson on M&T Swing link trucks. The trucks were replaced by Peckham P22s in about 1953. All were withdrawn in 1956.

241/42/44-46/49

Six cars were supplied in 1934 fitted with Metropolitan-Cammell steel bodies with domed roofs on M&T Swing link trucks. No 242 received a replacement P22 truck in about 1953. All were withdrawn between 1950 and 1952 with the exception of No 242 that survived until 1955.

During 1932 and 1933 Edinburgh acquired ten trams with bodywork produced by R. Y. Pickering, the only time that this Wishaw-based manufacturer supplied trams to the city. No 259 is pictured at Tollcross on 23 July 1951; at this date the car was still operating with its original M&T Swing-link four-wheel truck, but this was replaced later by a Peckham P22. Michael H. Waller

250-59

Supplied with bodies built by R. Y. Pickering of Wishaw on M&T Swing link trucks, this batch of ten cars was delivered during 1932 and 1933. No 256 was originally delivered with an English Electric FL32 truck, but this was transferred to No 267 when the latter was built in 1934. All bar No 255 received replacement P22 trucks in about 1953. The trams were withdrawn between 1952 and 1956.

260/61/65

These were three experimental cars delivered in 1933. Nos 260/65 were fitted with all-steel bodies supplied by Metropolitan-Cammell on M&T Swing link trucks, and No 261 had a mainly steel body constructed at Shrubhill on a Peckham P22. Nos 260/65 received replacement P22 trucks in about 1953. The three cars were withdrawn in 1955 (No 261) and 1956 (Nos 260/66).

Edinburgh No 260, seen here on route 10 at Toll Cross in August 1955, was one of two experimental cars supplied by Metropolitan-Cammell in 1933. By the date of this photograph the car had received a Peckham P22 in place of its original Maley & Taunton Swing-link truck. R. W. A. Jones/ Online Transport Archive (EH67)

Pictured at Granton Road station on a route 8 service to Newington is No 266; this car was originally numbered 371 when new in 1930 and survived in service until 1954. R. W. A. Jones/Online Transport Archive (EH14)

266

Originally numbered 371 when new in 1930 and renumbered in about 1933, No 266 had a fully enclosed Shrubhill-built body on an EMB hornless four-wheel truck. No 266 was withdrawn in 1954.

262/63/67

Delivered in 1934, this trio of cars was supplied with steel bodies built by English Electric on M&T Swing link four-wheel trucks, although No 267 initially was fitted with an English Electric FL32 truck. All were retrucked with Peckham P22s in about 1953 and were withdrawn during 1955 and 1956.

One of three cars supplied by English Electric on Maley & Taunton Swing-link trucks in 1934, No 262, seen here in August 1955 on route 14 (the Churchill Circle), had received a replacement Peckham P22 a couple of years earlier. No 262 survived in service until 1956. R. W. A. Jones/Online Transport Archive (EH65)

87, 90/92/93/95-99, 102/08/10/70/71, 270-311

These cars, all delivered in 1923, were fitted with open-balcony bodies supplied by the Bristol-based Leeds Forge on Peckham P22 four-wheel trucks. All were converted to fully enclosed between 1930 and 1933. The first to be delivered were Nos 270-311 with the remainder being replacements for withdrawn cable cars that had not been converted to electric traction. All were withdrawn between 1953 and 1955.

312-31

This batch of 20 open-balcony cars was delivered in 1924 with English Electric bodies on Peckham P22 trucks. All were fully enclosed between 1930 and 1933 and survived in service until withdrawal between 1952 and 1955.

332-70

Built between 1925 and 1930, these cars were fitted with bodies built at Shrubhill on Peckham P22 trucks. The early vehicles were supplied as open-balcony cars, but were fully enclosed between 1930 and 1933, with the last five, Nos 366-370, being delivered as fully enclosed. The batch was withdrawn between 1953 and 1956.

401-11

Edinburgh was the second Scottish operator to take advantage of the decision by Manchester Corporation to complete its tramway conversion programme in the late 1940s, acquiring 11 of the surplus 'Pilcher' cars between 1946 and 1948. Built originally between 1930 and 1932, the Edinburgh cars were originally Manchester Nos 173, 676, 196, 125, 558, 217, 389, 231, 242, 349 and 381 respectively. With bodies built in Manchester's own workshops, the cars were originally fitted with Peckham P35 trucks, although most had these replaced by, or modified to, P22 in Edinburgh. All were withdrawn by the end of 1954.

Ex-cable cars

Some 14 ex-cable cars that had been converted to electric traction in 1923 remained in service in 1945, although all were withdrawn by the end of 1947. They were replaced by new electric trams that had the same fleet numbers (see under Nos 32 etc above). Nos 210/17/19/24/25/28 dated originally to 1903 and originally had open-top Dick Kerr bodies that became open-balcony cars in 1907. Nos 73 and 172 (renumbered from Nos 27 and 25 respectively in 1933) dated from 1906, Nos 37 and 48 dated from 1907 and Nos 35, 49, 50 and 169 dated from 1908; these cars all had bodies built by the Edinburgh & District Tramways Co Ltd. All were originally built as balcony-top cars with the exception of No 169 that was built as open-top and converted to balcony-top. Although none of these converted cars survived into preservation, the body of sister car No 226 has been recovered and is currently undergoing restoration.

Works cars

Edinburgh employed a small fleet of dedicated works cars for works duties; these included seven salt cars. As with other operators, these were largely converted from erstwhile passenger trams.

EDINBURGH TRAMS

Operated by Edinburgh Trams Ltd, the single route – 8¾-mile (14km) in length – from Edinburgh Airport through to York Place opened to public service on 31 May 2014. Mired in controversy and vastly over budget, the one route section that has completed was part of a greater scheme that envisaged trams operating from the airport through the city centre and on to Leith and then back through Crewe Toll to Haymarket to create a loop. Proposed shortly after the Millennium, construction work commenced in 2008 but the time delay and massive over-spend led to the project almost being cancelled and to the decision not to proceed with the York Place-Leith-Haymarket section, although this is now again under consideration.

Edinburgh Trams Depot

There is a single depot serving the system, which is located to the north of the stop at Gogar.

Map of the Edinburgh Trams network as at 2015.

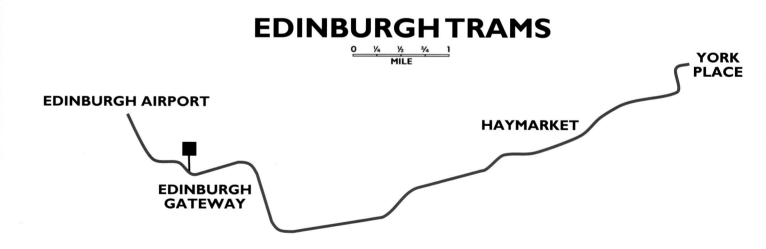

EDINBURGH TRAMS

0 ¼ ½ ¾ 1
MILE

YORK PLACE

EDINBURGH AIRPORT

HAYMARKET

EDINBURGH GATEWAY

After more than half a century, electric trams returned to Princes Street, Edinburgh, during 2014. Here one of the fleet of 27 Spanish-built trams heads westwards with a service to the airport. Gavin Booth

Edinburgh Trams Fleet

Although not actually entering service until 2014, the 27 trams built for the new Edinburgh system were constructed between 2009 and 2011 by CAF of Beasain, in Spain, at a cost of £40 million. The cars are numbered 251-77 and can accommodate up to 270 passengers, of which 78 are seated. The trams were specially designed to cope with the steep slopes associated with Edinburgh while ensuring low noise through a self-lubricating system to avoid tyre squeal on sharp curves.

GLASGOW

At the end of the Second World War, Glasgow possessed the largest tramway system in the British Isles. It possessed a fleet of some 1,200 cars, although relatively few were modern, and – courtesy of expanding over the lines of the Airdrie and Paisley companies – its operations spread well outside the city's boundaries. With the benefit of hindsight it is possible to see the seeds of the system's ultimate fate in those two facts – the age of the fleet and the operations beyond the boundaries – but at the time little seemed to threaten this great system. Indeed, such was the belief in the tram that in early 1945, Robert Bruce, the city engineer, produced a report on the future development of public transport in the city in which he stated that it 'would consist mainly of railed vehicles driven by electricity'. He foresaw the use of subways with single-deck cars and envisaged that the first stage would take place in 15 to 20 years.

Map of the Glasgow network as at 1945.

After the cessation of hostilities, little dramatic occurred. There were some minor route alterations in the summer of 1945: route 10 was revised to reverse at Hyndland Road; route 10A (a circular route via Church Street) was withdrawn; route 5 was also revised to reverse at Hyndland Road with alternative cars running via Botanic Gardens or Highburgh Road with a new crossover

Glasgow hex-dash
'Standard' No 128 stands at Burnside on 4 April 1948 awaiting departure with a route 18 service to Springburn.
Michael H. Waller

The scene at the Auchenshuggle terminus of route 9 to Dalmuir West on 23 March 1949 sees round-dash 'Standard' No 341 awaiting departure; some 13 years later, this particular route was destined to be the last converted to bus operation. Michael H. Waller

On 23 March 1949 'Standard' No 238 is pictured at Bishopbriggs with a service on route 25 to Carnwadric; the extension to Carnwadric was one of the few extensions completed in Scotland post-war. Michael H. Waller

Seen at the Renfrew Ferry terminus of route 28 to Glenfield is, appropriately, ex-Paisley car No 1053; this terminus was modified slightly in the late 1950s. Michael H. Waller

just short of the Kelvinside terminus; and route 16 now diverted to run via Elmbank Street rather than North Street, with the latter track now disused, via a new curve fitted with an electric point at the junction of Bothwell Street and Elmbank Street. Also in 1945 the construction of a new single-ended car – destined to be No 1005 – had been approved, and work repairing the railway bridge at Finnieston had required trams to operate over 100 yards of single track temporarily.

However, towards the end of the year *Modern Tramway* reported 'news of a similarly disquieting nature'; the news was that the general manager, E. R. L. Fitzpayne, had proposed the experimental conversion of route 2 (between Provanmill and Aikenhead Road) to trolleybus operation. He also proposed the abandonment of the Clydebank to Duntocher route, which required the use of single-deck cars, and the section from Broomhouse to Uddingston. There was also a proposal to see night trams replaced by buses with an increase in fares from 1d to 3d (this was rejected by the Traffic Commissioners early in 1946 unless the maximum fare was 2d). Despite these proposals,

Fitzpayne remained adamant that the tram remained central to Glasgow's transport provision and this was reflected early in 1946 by the agreement to purchase 100 new trams (although the experimental use of trolleybuses also remained on the agenda). Although the cost for 100 bogie trams was greater than that for an equivalent of four-wheel cars, Fitzpayne argued the committee 'might decide that only the best was good enough for Glasgow'. Approval was also given in early 1946 for the extension of the Knightswood route to South Drumry at a cost of £26,000. Also during 1946, a fares increase was implemented on 18 August that resulted in a 4d maximum on the trams. In addition, revised traffic control at Eglinton Toll resulted in the creation of two separate highways and the consequent diversion of routes 5, 5A, 11, 14 and 24 the same day. This diversion was not popular with regular passengers whose journeys had been adversely affected.

The following year was relatively quiet, although in the late summer a new quarter-mile branch to serve the housing estate at Carnwadric from Boydstone Road at Thornliebank was

On 24 March 1949, 'Coronation' No 1238 stands at the then Spiersbridge terminus of route 14; with the withdrawal of trams on route 28 between Cross Stobs and Glenfield in early April, service No 14 was extended beyond Spiersbridge to serve Cross Stobs. Until 1923 and Glasgow's takeover of the tram operations of Paisley District Tramways Co, there was no physical connection between the two systems at Spiersbridge. Michael H. Waller

Glasgow experimented with the Ultimate-style ticket system from 1948 and this is one of five ticket values known to have been issued in the first series produced that year. Author's Collection

The Ultimate system gradually replaced the TIM machines in use previously and all the latter were largely superseded by the end of 1953. This TIM was issued towards the end of this period, on 7 April 1953, on route 32 (Crookston to Bishopbriggs). Author's Collection

The scene in Newlands Depot after the disastrous fire of 1948. Michael H. Waller

proposed and, later in the year, powers were formally granted to permit the operation of trolleybuses in the city. These plans were not considered a serious threat to the existing tram network as no trunk tram route was threatened and the new trolleybuses were also expected to serve areas beyond the tram termini. Mention has already been made of the age of the fleet and the number of routes outside the city's boundaries; by the late 1940s another major problem also emerged – the transport department's

financial position. During the financial year ended 31 March 1946, the trams and buses lost about £130,000 each and, in mid-1948, the estimated loss to 31 March 1949 was £400,000 and that the total debt to 31 March 1948 was already £1 million. Fare increases were again implemented during the summer of 1948 but, increasingly, more radical solutions were deemed necessary. In the summer of 1948 Fitzpayne proposed that, although the core tramway network be preserved (indeed be invested in as the idea of

subways remained a possibility), the more outlying sections be converted to trolleybus operation.

The tramcar fleet reached its peak in 1948, with 1,200 in service, but these were to be reduced following the disastrous fire in Newlands Depot on 11 April 1948. This resulted in the loss of a number of 'Standard' and 'Coronation' cars, although the latter were repaired or rebuilt; the first to be repaired was No 1239. The insurance payment received allowed for the construction of eight replacement 'Coronation' cars – 1255/79/393-98 – during 1954 and 1955; Nos 1393-98 were constructed using EMB trucks acquired second-hand from Liverpool. More positively, the year witnessed the introduction of the first of the post-war 'Cunarder' cars with deliveries from the summer running at two per week from Coplawhill Works. Also positive was the opening of the branch to Carnwadric; this commenced operation as route 14B

on 7 April 1948 with a 12min headway. The long-foreshadowed withdrawal of the outer section of route 29 from Broomhouse to Uddingston, however, took place on 28 August 1948. There was a slight extension on 3 October 1948 when a new siding serving route 4 to Renfrew South opened. This extended for about a quarter of a mile along Porterfield Road.

Glasgow's plans for introducing trolleybuses were gathering pace. On 23 January 1949 buses replaced trams on the Oatlands to Townhead section of route 10 and were scheduled to replace trams temporarily on routes 2 (Provanmill to Polmadie) and 19 (Muirend to Springburn) to permit the erection of trolleybus overhead (these conversions actually took place on 20 February 1949). These changes resulted in the following route alterations, although little track was actually abandoned at this stage: route 10 and new route 36 now operated between Kelvinside and Parkhead Cross

The section of route 28 between Glenfield and Cross Stobs, which was largely single track with passing loops, was abandoned on 2 April 1949. On 24 March 1949, shortly before the abandonment of the route south from here, ex-Paisley No 1063 stands at Glenfield with a service to Renfrew Ferry. Michael H. Waller

On 24 March 1949, some nine months before the route was converted to bus operation, four single-deck trams sit at the terminus of route 20 at Duntocher. No 923 was one of five 'Standard' double-deckers cut down for use as single-deck cars in 1939. No 1009 was one of 17 of the ex-Paisley cars converted to single-deck in 1924/25 for use on the Duntocher route. Five of the latter had been withdrawn before the Second World War to be replaced by the converted 'Standard' cars. Michael H. Waller

by two alternative routes; route 34 and new route 35 ran between Dennistoun and Rutherglen via either Bridgeton Cross or Parkhead Cross; alternate cars on route 26 diverted at Rutherglen to serve Oatlands; and route 30 was curtailed to Dalmarnock from Cambuslang. These were followed on 20 February 1949 by the renumbering of the Carnwadric service as the 31. Also in early 1949 work started on the extension to the Knightswood route; any further extension was, however, difficult due to the canal bridge beyond the new terminus. The first of the new trolleybuses commenced operation on 3 April 1949; Glasgow was the last wholly new trolleybus operator in the UK and the only system to commence operation post-war.

The previous day saw the abandonment of the semi-rural single-track section of route 28 between Cross Stobbs and Glenfield. This resulted in the 28 running between Glenfield and Renfrew Ferry only.

On 31 July 1949 the Knightswood extension on reserved track to Blairdardie opened; it was served by an extension to the existing route 30. The extension westwards from Blairdardie to Duntocher was authorised but, in the event, was never constructed as a result of the bridge over the Forth & Clyde Canal immediately to the west of the new terminus. This was destined to be the last extension opened in Glasgow. By this date, however, construction of the new 'Cunarder' cars was progressing and by the date of the extension's opening, new cars up to No 1304 had been delivered. The Blairdardie extension was offset later in the year when, on 3 December, the long foreshadowed conversion of route 20 (Clydebank to Duntocher) took place. The tram fleet at the end of December stood at 1,190 (alongside 703 buses and 34 trolleybuses).

The following year was relatively quiet. There were no service conversions while construction of the 'Cunarder' cars continued, with all up to No 1369 being in service by 31 December. The year also saw relatively few service alterations. The most significant of these was the restoration of through services on route 12 from Linthouse to Mount Florida on 15 March. These had been suspended on 1 May 1949 when work needed on the railway bridge at Strathbungo required the cessation of tram operation.

Temporary crossovers were laid at either side and the route was thus operated in two halves until the bridge was reopened. The year was, however, marked by an accident when, on 24 May, a bus skidded and was hit by a tram heading for Dalmuir West. Seven were killed and 40 injured on the bus; there were no casualties on the tram. The end of the year witnessed a further increase in fares, with the minimum fare increased from 1d to 1½d. That the future of the tram system was now subject to some debate was emphasised on 21 December when the council voted by a majority of only two to send back a proposal for the conversion of the system to trolleybus operation for further consideration. To counter the increasing anti-tram rhetoric, the Scottish Division of the LRTL produced a report advocating major work to improve the network.

With the unopened extension to Blairdairdie stretching into the distance, Glasgow 'Standard' No 264 stands at the Knightswood terminus of route 30 on 19 June 1949. Michael H. Waller

On 1 July 1951 Glasgow route 13 was extended from Maryhill to Milngavie to cover for route 11 – Sinclair Drive to Milngavie – that was withdrawn on that date. Here 'Standard' No 152 stands at Milngavie with a service to Mount Florida. The 13 ceased operation on 2 August 1953 when the 29 was extended to Milngavie to compensate. R. W. A. Jones/ Online Transport Archive (GL23)

The following year, 1951, was also relatively quiet with no service conversions until later in the year and construction of the new 'Cunarder' cars still ongoing. By the end of the year, production had reached 1391 leaving just one of the batch – No 1392 – to be delivered in 1952; it finally entered service on 12 February 1952. The last cars to be completed – Nos 1388-93 – were delayed due to late delivery of components. There were a number of service modifications. On 4 March route 34 became a service linking Auchenshuggle with Anderston Cross rather than Alexandra Park, and the next day route 40 was extended to Dumbreck from Ibrox on weekdays between 4 pm and 6 pm (this partially reversed the service curtailment of 7 May 1950 when the route was cut back to Ibrox from Dumbreck). On 1 April, as a result of the doubling of the short street of single track between the terminus at Keppochill Road and Springburn

Road, routes 4 and 16 were extended from Keppochhill Road to Springburn Road (Elmvale Street). On 1 July 1951, in connection with the introduction of trolleybuses to Gorbals, routes 5 and 24 were diverted between Renfield Street and Eglinton Toll. At the same time route 11, from Sinclair Drive to Milngavie, was withdrawn, being replaced by the extension of route 13 from Maryhill to Milngavie and by the partial diversion of cars terminating at Langside on route 24 to serve Sinclair Drive. The partial diversion of the 24 lasted until 5 August when all cars reverted to the Langside terminus and Sinclair Drive was served by a new service, 24A, that linked Kelvingrove with Sinclair Drive. This new arrangement was not to last long; on 2 December the 24A was replaced by buses resulting in the abandonment of the Sinclair Drive section from its junction with Battlefield Road. The end of the year again saw an increase in fares.

The last of the 'Cunarder' cars was delivered in early 1952, completing the order for 100 new cars. No 1392 was the last wholly new double-deck tram to be constructed in Britain; on withdrawal it was preserved. Elsewhere work continued on the development of the trolleybus network with trolleybus standards erected on route 13 to Clarkston in the spring. Trolleybus operation commenced between Cathedral Street and Muirend station on 31 August 1952, replacing the southern part of bus route 37, although tram route 13 remained operational. Part of the equipment used on the trolleybus extension was salvaged by cutting back route 9 by two-thirds of a mile from Carmyle to Auchenshuggle; this was the only section of route abandoned during the year. Other service changes saw, on 4 May, the incorporation of route 34 (Anderston Cross to Auchenshuggle) into the 9; on 5 May 1952, the withdrawal of all services between Baillieston and Airdrie on route 23 except between 7 am and 9 am and 4.30 pm and 6.30 pm on weekdays; and, on 2 November 1952, the extension of bus route 37 south from Pollokshaws to Nether Auldhouse Road. Fares were again increased during the year, this time from 5 October, and the end of the year was marred by two serious accidents. On 28 November 1952, 'Standard' No 390 overturned while operating on the 27, killing its driver and injuring the conductress and four passengers, and on 8 December 1952, No 6 (one of the cars built after the Blitz of 1941) collided with Nos 1280/82 at Renfrew; this time, however, there were no injuries and No 6 was repaired and returned to service in mid-1953.

'Standard' No 883 stands at the terminus of route 9 at Carmyle on 23 March 1949; the route was cut back by two-thirds of a mile to Causewayside Street on 15 June 1952. Some of the overhead recovered was used in the extension of the city's new trolleybus system. Note the use of the colour route band between the decks; the use of such bands remained a feature of Glasgow tram operation in the post-war years. Michael H. Waller

In early 1953 it was announced that Glasgow was to acquire 24 ex-Liverpool bogie cars. In all, 46 were eventually acquired, all entering service during 1953 and 1954. One is seen here heading towards Maryhill on route 29.
John B. McCann/ Online Transport Archive (114-26)

On 22 March 1949 'Standard' No 683 stands at Bishopbriggs on the long route 32 service to Elderslie. The 32 was cut back from Bishopbriggs to Springburn on 2 August 1953.
Michael H. Waller

The New Year witnessed more positive news: a sub-committee of the transport committee rejected a proposal that operation of trams outside the city's boundaries should cease in favour of buses from Scottish Omnibuses, and Glasgow was to acquire 24 of the streamlined bogie cars from Liverpool at £500 apiece. Less positive, however, was the decision to withdraw the trams to Clarkston in favour of the new trolleybuses. To facilitate the introduction of trolleybus route 105 (Clarkston to Firhill), a number of route changes were effected on 4 July 1953: route 5 was cut back from Clarkston to Holmlea Road; route 13 was diverted to operate from Milngavie to Glasgow Cross via Hope Street and Argyle Street; and route 23 was diverted between Queen's Cross and St Vincent Street to eliminate all trams from operation along West Nile Street. These changes were required as a consequence of Ministry of Transport regulations concerning the operation of bow-collector trams alongside trolleybuses. That trams were still perceived as having a future was emphasised in a comment by the general manager; Fitzpayne stated: 'It is likely that we shall keep them for some time to come – we shall not recklessly throw away useful assets.'

On 2 August 1953 route 32 trams were cut back from Bishopbriggs to terminate at Springburn (Elmvale Street) due to congestion at the original terminus. On 4 November route 29 from Broomhouse to Anderston Cross was extended to Milngavie, partly in replacement for the remaining section of the route 13, which ceased to operate, and partly to create a new cross-city route for the ex-LCPT trams. On the same day a number of short workings on route 14 were extended from Spiersbridge to a new crossover at Arden. At the end of the year, the go-ahead was given to lift 15 miles of track from sections that had been abandoned; one of the first sections to be removed was part of Renfield Street north of Sauchiehall Street. Among other track lifted was a section in South Portland Street that had been laid in 1923 with a view to a new – but unbuilt – bridge across the river and which, therefore, was never used.

The first of the ex-Liverpool cars – No 927 (late Glasgow No 1024; its condition was such that it took longer to prepare for service) – arrived in September 1953; the estimated cost was £100 to prepare each of the cars for service and that they would have a life of 20 years. The first of the type, No 1006 (ex-Liverpool No 942), entered service on 16 October 1953 on route 29 and was allocated to Maryhill depot. The trucks of the cars were delivered first for conversion from standard to 4ft 7¾in-gauge. Apart from refurbishing these cars, Coplawhill was also building the replacement 'Coronation' cars, Nos 1393-98, using second-hand bogies acquired from Liverpool earlier, on more spartan bodies to reduce the cost. In early 1954 authorisation to purchase a further 13 ex-Liverpool cars was given; this was subsequently increased to 22 and in all 46 of the type migrated northwards. The second batch cost £500 plus £80 transport each and were delivered from late summer onwards; initially they were stored at Newlands Depot on delivery as Coplawhill was engaged in other work with the first of the new 'Coronation' cars entering service on 6 July 1954.

Early 1954 witnessed further service alterations. On 7 February route 4 was extended from Renfrew South to Paisley North, and on the same day the terminus of routes 29 and 40 were relocated in Maryhill from the terminal stub in Caldercuilt Road (which was abandoned at this date) to a new crossover in Maryhill Road. On 9 May 1954 the Sunday service of route 40 was amended to run between Maryhill and Douglas Street only; this change was not to last long as the Sunday service over the route was withdrawn entirely on 22 August 1954.

By the middle of 1954 the future of the tram system was not as secure as it might have been. In the spring Fitzpayne produced a report in which he advocated extending the trolleybus network while reducing the tram fleet to 800 to eliminate the oldest surviving 'Standard' cars. On 1 June 1954, at a private meeting of the Labour group, it was decided not to replace 450 of the oldest trams; when details of the meeting were reported in the *Glasgow Herald*, the newspaper commented that this represented the first step towards abandonment. Despite this, work on the system continued; the complex junction of Renfield Street with Sauchiehall Street was relaid overnight during 14/15 August, and a new terminal layout at Renfrew Ferry was brought into use on 27 August 1954. A new terminal stub at Hillcroft Terrace, Colston, was constructed; this was used from 10 October 1954 when route 25 was cut back from Bishopbriggs to Colston. Other route changes on 10 October 1954 were: the diversion of route 17 from Cambuslang to serve Anniesland rather than Anderston Cross or Whiteinch; the cutting back of route 21 from Anniesland to St Vincent Street; the cessation of operation of route 23 beyond Baillieston to Airdrie; and the change of route 32 from Elderslie to Springburn to become Crookstown to Bishopbriggs (effectively replacing the 25 on the section from Colston to Bishopbriggs). At the end of 1954, some 1,067 trams were in stock, of which 872 were required for a full service.

On 3 December 1954 the extension to Pinxston power station, which had cost £2 million, was formally opened. Still corporation owned, the possession of its own generating station was a powerful incentive to the retention of electrically powered vehicles in the city. As a result, on 26 November 1954, the council rejected a Labour plan to replace 450 old trams with buses; the new policy was to see the elimination of the trams but their replacement by trolleybuses as well as buses. The plan envisaged the fleet being reduced to 750 over a four-year period. In early 1955 Fitzpayne reported on the plan approved in November; he anticipated that the following – routes 4, 5/5A, 21, 22, 24, 27, 28 and 32 – would be converted to bus and the 7 and 12 would be converted to trolleybus. Of the 450 obsolete cars, 150 had already been withdrawn with a number replaced by the ex-Liverpool bogie cars. By the end of the process, he believed there would be a system of 18 routes operated by 700 trams. In the meantime, work was in hand on the preparation of the remaining Liverpool trams for service. The council approved Fitzpayne's plans on 14 April.

On 20 March 1955, following numerous complaints, route 25 trams were re-extended from the new terminus at Colston to Bishopbriggs; the new siding at Colston was thereafter used by the PW Department. On 7 August 1955 the section between Shawfield and Rutherglen Cross along Main Street, Rutherglen was abandoned to permit the erection of trolleybus overhead for route 101. This affected routes 18 and 26. The former were diverted to run to Burnside via Dalmarnock, and those serving Rutherglen were terminated at Shawfield and showed new route 18A; those cars from Shawfield to Springburn continued to show simply route 18. With the 26, those cars that served Oatlands were cut back to terminate at Shawfield and were given the new route number 26A; in the reverse direction, heading towards Scotstoun, all cars still showed 26. Approval was given in autumn 1955 for the purchase of 36 buses; these were required to facilitate the conversion of routes 5/5A and 24; expenditure of £33,000 on new trolleybus overhead and a further £30,000 for five new double-deck trolleybuses was also approved. A factor determining the future of transport in the Glasgow area at this time was the question of the extensive suburban railway network; the Inglis Report of 1951 had recommended the electrification of much of the network, and the British Transport Commission and Glasgow Corporation held discussions as to how the programme – estimated to cost £13.5 million – could be implemented. Effectively a bargain was struck – the suburban lines would be electrified but the tram network would be sacrificed as a consequence. Approved by the BTC in 1956, work started on the scheme in early 1957. From a corporation standpoint, the investment had the added advantage of guaranteeing work for Pinxston, where a considerable sum had recently been invested.

On 2 February 1956 the council agreed to cease the operation of a number of routes outside the city boundaries. The decision was not welcomed by those authorities outside the city that would be affected; two members of Paisley Council, for example, suggested that Paisley should take over the operation of the trams within its boundaries. On 18 March there was a further revision to the fares; the minimum fare increased from 2d to 2½d. On 8 April route 31 from Lambhill to Pollokshaws was diverted to run via Kilmarnock Road and terminate at Merrylee Road rather than at Nether Auldhouse Road in Pollokshaws.

On 29 April 1956 route 1 was curtailed from Dalmuir West to Scotstoun West except at peak hours (Monday–Friday until 8.30 am and 4 pm to 6.30 pm, and Sundays until 8.30 am and from 3 pm to 5 pm); this change was partially reversed on 7 May 1956 when cars were extended to Yoker between noon and 2 pm. A new crossover was installed at Richmond Park Laundry, on Cambuslang Road, to permit route 17 to be cut back from Cambuslang to Farme Cross; this change was effected on 3 November 1956. By this stage withdrawals of 'Standard' cars was running at about ten per week and, following the closure of Langside depot on 29 September, the tramcar fleet was reduced to fewer than 1,000. Despite the reduction in the size of the system, there was still, however, no appetite for complete conversion; on 13 September 1956 the council voted 50-20 against the complete abandonment of the system.

A 'Coronation' car stands at the modified terminus at Renfrew Ferry; evidence of the former layout can be seen to the left of the tram. Services over the Renfrew Ferry to Glenfield section – route 28 – were withdrawn on 11 May 1957 with the abandonment of services in Paisley. This service was known as the 'Goldmine' due to its high frequency.
R. W. A. Jones/Online Transport Archive (GL83)

The section of line beyond Baillieston to Airdrie was withdrawn on 3 November 1956; that and the section of the 14 converted earlier were not replaced by corporation buses. Here two 'Standard' cars, with No 499 leading, await departure from the terminus at Airdrie. Route 23 had operated beyond Baillieston until 10 October 1954. No 499 is bound for Coatbridge depot; cars on short-workings displayed split numbers as shown here. R. W. A. Jones/Online Transport Archive (GL38)

The process of abandoning sections of route outside the city boundaries was, however, to progress. On 29 September 1956 the section of route 14 from Arden to Cross Stobs was abandoned; this was followed on 3 November by the cessation of tram operation on route 15 between Baillieston and Airdrie along with the Airdrie to Coatbridge local service (with the consequent closure of the tram depot in Coatbridge; the corporation gave Airdrie Council £42,250 in 1959 to fund the removal of track and the reinstatement of roads), the aforementioned curtailment of route 17 and the section of route 29 between Maryhill Park and Milngavie. The last car to traverse the section to Airdrie was 'Coronation' No 1251. One consequence of the curtailment of route 29 at Maryhill was that the Monday-Saturday route 40 could be withdrawn on the same day; this withdrawal did not, however, result in any track being abandoned. Following

these changes, the tram fleet was further reduced and now totalled 308 modern cars, 49 older bogie cars, 512 'Standard' cars plus single-deck No 1089 and driver-training car No 1017. In addition there were 35 works cars and trailers; 12 of the former had been fitted with electrical equipment salvaged from passenger cars withdrawn over the previous 12 months.

The end of 1956 saw Glasgow, as elsewhere in Britain, hit by the fuel restrictions that resulted from the Suez Crisis. This delayed the conversion of the routes in Paisley and resulted in Airdrie Council voting on 6 December 1956 to seek the restoration of tram services during the period of fuel shortages; this request was not acceded to. Between 30 November and 1 December 1956 cars running southbound on routes 5 and 24 were diverted to run via Pollokshaws Road and the school car training line in Coplaw Street due to subsidence at Eglinton Toll. As a result of the fuel crisis,

all-night tram services were introduced to routes 1, 9, 16, 19 and 23; with the easing of restrictions, these all-night services were all withdrawn on 30 March 1957.

In early 1957 the corporation rejected a request from Renfrew Council that trams continue to serve the area after the conversion of the routes in Paisley. A public enquiry into the conversion in Paisley was held over five days in February 1957 but, with the end of fuel restrictions during the same month, the corporation announced that the Paisley

routes would now be converted on 12 May rather than the proposed date of July. The licences to operate the replacement buses had still not, however, been granted. On 10 February 1957, routes 15 and 23 were shortened slightly at Baillieston by the use of a new crossover at Martin Crescent. This meant that trams no longer had to cross the busy A8, although the eastbound track continued in use for some time by cars going for scrap, which were uplifted on the former reserved track by scrap merchant Connells of Coatbridge.

Ex-Paisley car No 1069, similar to No 1068 that was eventually preserved, is pictured on Coplaw Street; this track was not generally used for passenger cars but was pressed into service on 30 November 1956 when subsidence at Eglinton Toll caused passenger cars on routes 5 and 24 to be diverted via Coplaw Street overnight.
R. W. A. Jones (GL30)

The terminus at Baillieston was slightly relocated on 10 February 1957; on 30 December 1958 'Coronation' No 1279, one of those built in 1954, stands at the new terminus with a route 23 service to Maryhill.
Hamish Stevenson/ Online Transport Archive (706)

'Standard' No 160 is outside Elderslie depot; this depot, inherited from Paisley District Tramways Co on 1 August 1923, was to lose its services, after some delay as a consequence of the Suez Crisis. Routes in Paisley were finally abandoned on 11 May 1957. R. W. A. Jones/Online Transport Archive (GL16)

On 11 May 1957, following the granting of the bus licences at the end of April, the long-foreshadowed conversion of the routes to Paisley took effect; this resulted in the withdrawal of routes 21 and 28 and the curtailment of routes 4 and 27 at Hillington Road. The last car to serve Paisley was 'Coronation' No 1277. These withdrawals resulted in the closure of Elderslie depot and its associated yard where condemned trams had been scrapped. The last car to be dealt with at Elderslie was 'Standard' No 847 on 9 May 1957. Elderslie's allocation of 'Coronation' cars was transferred to Dalmarnock and 50 surplus 'Standard' cars were sold for scrap to Connell of Coatbridge.

It was expected that the next services to be converted would be routes 5, 5A and 24, which were all based at Langside depot, in October 1957. Early summer witnessed the removal of the final overhead in Paisley and the lifting of the reserved track between Bailieston and Langloan. The disused but intact track along the reserved section west of Arden on the Cross Stobbs route was also lifted, with the land released to the Housing Department.

On 24 June 1957 the general manager produced a report for the Transport Committee; in it Fitzpayne argued for the replacement of all older trams and that the entire system, given the age profile of the more modern cars, be converted over a twenty-year period.

Routes 5 and 5A
– from Holmlea
Road to Kelvinside
– were withdrawn
on 16 November
1957; on the last
day, No 658 stands
at Holmlea Road.
Hamish Stevenson/
Online Transport
Archive (115)

He estimated the costs of replacing 564 older cars at £11.23m for trams, £7.412m for trolleybuses and £5.539m for buses. The twenty-year period was longer than mooted elsewhere, where a maximum of four years was one suggestion.

The crossover at Merrylee was moved 180 yards south with services on route 31 being cut back to this point from 18 August 1957; on the same date route 23 services were extended from Gairbraid Avenue to Maryhill. Maryhill was the

Route 27 – from
Shieldhall to
Springburn – was
withdrawn on
15 March 1958,
although the
withdrawal resulted
in no track being
abandoned. On 26
December 1957
'Standard' No 674 is
seen on Govan Road
heading towards
Shieldhall. Hamish
Stevenson/Online
Transport Archive (131)

scene of a collision on 7 September 1957 when 'Coronation' No 1287 collided with a lorry, but there were no casualties and the tram remained in service; a more serious accident had occurred the previous month when ex-Liverpool No 1042 was badly damaged. The estimated cost of repair, plus the relatively poor condition of the car, led to the decision to withdraw it; this was the first of the ex-Liverpool cars to be taken out of service.

The fate of the tramway system was effectively sealed on 25 September 1957 when the Labour group on the council agreed in principle that complete conversion be party policy. As if to demonstrate that the future of the trams was now uncertain, on the following day 'Standard' No 658 escaped from Partick depot and ran under its own power, but without crew, for a distance along Dumbarton Road.

The next conversions took place on 16 November 1957 when routes 5 and 5A were converted to bus operation; this was to have been followed on 8 January 1958 by the conversion of route 24. In the event the latter conversion was delayed until 15 March 1958. Also converted on 15 March was route 27, Shieldhall to Springburn via Saracen Street, although this conversion did not result in any track abandonment. The conversion of routes 24 and 27 allowed for the withdrawal of 25 cars, which were sold for scrap to Bird and dismantled on a siding installed at Colston in 1954, on the Bishopbriggs route. However, after five cars had been so treated, objections from the police and fire service, concerned about the fire risk, resulted in the surviving cars being resold to Connell of Coatbridge. The cars destined for Coatbridge went initially to Baillieston before completing their journeys by road.

On 1 December 1957, 'Cunarder' No 1352 stands at the terminus of route 7 at Bellahouston; this service was replaced by trolleybus service 106 and operated for the last time with trams on 14 June 1958. Hamish Stevenson/ Online Transport Archive (136)

More positive news, however was that No 1003, which had been seriously damaged in an accident on Govan Road on 29 November 1957, had been rebuilt and restored to traffic. Route 16 was transferred from Possilpark depot to Partick on 16 March 1958; this resulted in the operation of 'Coronation' cars on the route for the first time. Work continued on the next conversions, routes 7 and 12. Route 7 was replaced by trolleybus route 106 on 14 June 1958 and work was quickly undertaken to replace some of the junctions used by the route with plain track; the track in Cumbernauld Road, however, survived to permit access for cars on routes 6 and 8 to Dennistoun depot. A batch of 21 'Cunarders' was transferred from Govan to Dalmarnock for use on routes 9, 10, 17, 18 and 26; this resulted in the regular appearance of this type of car on Argyle Street for the first time.

That the life of Glasgow's once massive system was fast ebbing away was confirmed in late summer 1958; a loss of £577,000 in the previous year led to the announcement that the process of abandonment was to be speeded up. As if to indicate the change of policy, when 'Coronation' No 1289 was derailed and overturned at the junction of Gallowgate and Springfield Road on 21 July 1958, the decision was made not to repair the car, although it was not officially withdrawn until January 1959. Between 1 May and 31 October 1958 no fewer than 95 passenger trams and six works cars were scrapped. These were followed by a further 132 between 1 November 1958 and 15 April 1959. These losses included the five non-standard 'Lightweight' cars, Nos 6, 1001-04, that were disposed of in February 1959. All trams were now being dismantled at Coplawhill with the wooden bodies burnt.

On 15 November
1958 route 12 from Mount Florida to Paisley Road Toll was withdrawn, being converted into trolleybus route 108. On 3 July 1958, 'Standard' No 585, which was later preserved, stands at the Mount Florida terminus.
Hamish Stevenson/ Online Transport Archive (348)

The 17 – from Farme Cross to Anniesland – was another route converted on 15 November 1958; here 'Standard' No 22, which was later preserved, is seen at the junction of Argyle Street and Union Street with a service for Farme Cross on 31 October 1958. *Hamish Stevenson/Online Transport Archive (607)*

The third route converted on 15 November 1958 was the 22 from Crookston to Lambhill; here 'Standard' No 160 heads to Lambhill along Gower Street on 31 October 1958. *Hamish Stevenson/Online Transport Archive (608)*

Alongside these withdrawals, the conversion programme continued apace. On 6 September 1958 route 4 was converted to bus operation; this resulted in the track between Lorne Street and Shieldhall being retained solely for the use of peak-hour cars on route 12. This peak-hour extension survived until 14 November 1958 and, when withdrawn, resulted in trams ceasing to serve Govan. This was followed the next day by the conversion of routes 12, 17, 22 and 32. Route 12 was replaced by trolleybus service 108, and route 17, from Anniesland to Farme Cross, was abandoned without replacement as an economy measure; route 26A was diverted at Bridgeton Cross from

Shawfield to Farme Cross in partial replacement. This service became linked with the 26 on 16 November; the new 26 became Clydebank/Scotstoun to Burnside/Farme Cross. To compensate for the loss of route 32 cars operating between Springburn and Bishopbriggs, extra trams were allocated to route 25. These closures rendered 70 cars surplus; these were stored at Govan depot pending disposal. These conversions –along with

that of route 8 –would have represented the end of the original conversion plan. The system's route mileage was now 75, of which 12 miles remained outside the city's boundaries. A second 'Coronation', No 1152, was damaged in a collision, on Cumbernauld Road, in which its driver, John Russell, was killed. A second fatal accident occurred on 28 January 1959 when 'Coronation' No 1145 collided with a lorry on Shettleston Road; the driver

The final route converted on 15 November 1958 was the 32 from Crookston to Bishopbriggs; on 31 October 1958, 'Standard' No 301 heads along Paisley Road with a service to Crookston. Hamish Stevenson/Online Transport Archive (615)

Route 8 – from Millerston to Rouken Glen – was converted on 14 March 1959; this abandonment also resulted in the temporary loss of the Rouken Glen circular as the service was linked with the 25 that was to survive for a further three months. On 8 March 1959, 'Standard' No 24 stands at the Millerston terminus along with No 464, which was in use on an LRTL special. Hamish Stevenson/ Online Transport Archive (757)

Carnwadric was one of the post-war extensions, being opened on 7 November 1948, but services on route 25, from Carnwadric/Rouken Glen to Bishopbriggs, were converted on 6 June 1959. On the last day an impressive line-up of cars at Carnwadric sees a 'Coronation' – No 1222 – plus two 'Standards' – Nos 103 and 209 – awaiting their next duties. Hamish Stevenson/Online Transport Archive (1012)

The Springburn circular – route 33 – was converted on 2 May 1959; on the last day 'Standard' No 48 is pictured on Bilsland Road heading for Springburn. Hamish Stevenson/Online Transport Archive (932)

and two passengers died. These were the first passenger fatalities on Glasgow's trams since 1942.

On 4 January the closure of a bridge on Eldon Street, which required replacement, led to closure of the University section; as a result the 3 was diverted from the University to Park Road and the 14 to Kelvingrove (Radnor Street). The last of the services originally scheduled to be converted, route 8, was converted to bus operation on 14 March 1959; at the same time cars on route 25 were extended to the crossover at Milverton Road that had previously been the terminus of route 8. The conversion of route 8 temporarily resulted in the end of the Rouken Glen circular; this situation pertained until 6 June 1959 when route 25 was converted to bus operation. The conversion of route 25 included the section to Carnwardric that had opened on 7 November 1948; this had been the last first-generation street tramway to be completed in Britain. On 2 May 1959 route 33 – the Springburn circular – became the next casualty.

Following the fatal accident and fire on No 1145, all the surviving post-war cars were fitted with a new emergency switch. The first to be so treated was No 1222, with the modification being completed thereafter at a rate of five per week. A further indication that the tramway system was living on borrowed time came with the closure, again during the summer, of the driver training school at Coplawhill. This rendered No 1017 redundant, although it continued in use as a occasional shunter thereafter. Between 15 April and 18 September 1959, 105 passenger cars were scrapped; the majority were 'Standard' cars but a number of the ex-Liverpool cars also succumbed. On 6 September 1959 route 16 was cut back from Springburn to its earlier Keppochhill Road terminus. Springburn was served by trams on route 18 and by a number of bus services. Another indication of the tramway's

fate came in the autumn of 1959; the relaying of the track at the junction of Eglinton Street and Bridge Street was the last occasion on which thermit welding was used. Thereafter, future trackwork would be provided with fishplates to make removal easier after closure. On 7 September 1959, as a result of work on the bridge over the Forth & Clyde Canal at Dalmuir, services to Dalmuir West on routes 1 and 9 were terminated 600 yards short of the terminus at

On 6 June 1959, 'Coronation' No 1248 heads along Parliamentary Road with a route 6 service for Scotstoun; this service was converted to bus operation on 31 October 1959. Hamish Stevenson/ Online Transport Archive (1008)

Also converted on 31 October 1959 was route 14 from Kelvingrove to Arden; on 6 June 1959, 'Coronation' No 1219 is pictured in Thornliebank with a service heading towards Kelvingrove. *Hamish Stevenson/ Online Transport Archive (1016)*

'Cunarder' No 1347 crosses the swing bridge at Dalmuir with an enthusiasts' tour; work on this bridge resulted in the suspension of trams over it between 7 September 1959 and 1 August 1960. *R. W. A. Jones/Online Transport Archive (GL11)*

Dalmuir; this curtailment continued until 1 August 1960 when services on route 9 were re-extended to the original terminus with 'Kilmarnock Bogie' No 1092 being the first over the reopened section. On 1 November routes 6 and 14 were replaced by buses; this meant that there were now only two services serving the southern half of the city: route 3 (Mosspark) and 31 (Lambhill-Merrylee). The latter was, however, not to last much longer as, on 5 December 1959, it was abandoned unexpectedly without replacement; originally routes 3 and 31 were planned to be among the last routes to close.

Routes 1 and 30 – Dalmarnock to Scotstoun West and Dalmarnock to Blairdardie respectively – were both converted on 12 March 1960. On 20 June 1959 'Standards' Nos 113 (on the 30) and 65 (on the 1) head along Springfield Road. Hamish Stevenson/ Online Transport Archive (1060)

By 1 March 1960, the passenger fleet had been reduced to just 403 cars, of which 95 were 'Standards'. Only six of the ex-Liverpool cars – Nos 1012/16/25/33/36/55 – remained. Most remaining 'Standard' cars were all scheduled to be withdrawn following the conversion of routes 1 and 30 on 12 March 1960; these were the last routes to be operated exclusively by 'Standard' cars as a sharp curve at Parkhead Cross precluded the use of more modern cars.

The last tram from Blairdardie – the last section of the Glasgow system to open (on 31 July 1949) – was 'Standard' No 9; it was also the last tram from Scotstoun West to Partick depot. Parkhead depot closed at the same time, with all cars removed except for collision casualty No 1295. Route 15 was now operated from Dennistoun, and a section of line in Springfield Road, used by routes 1 and 30, was retained to allow depot access to Dalmarnock.

It was announced that only seven routes – Nos 9, 15, 18, 18A, 26, 26A and 29 – were expected to survive beyond the end of 1960. However, a significant number of cars remained operational as a number of routes, such as the 9 and 29, required 50 trams each to maintain the service. It was also announced that the planned date for final closure had been brought forward from 1963 to 1962. The next service to be converted was route 3, which succumbed on 4 June 1960. The same day saw route 10 withdrawn without direct replacement, although services on route 9 were strengthened. The following day saw route 23 diverted between St Vincent Street and New City Road in the city centre to permit the removal of trams from Renfield Street, Sauchiehall Street and

Cambridge Street. With the conversion of route 3, the only sections of track that remained south of the river were those to the Permanent Way yard at Barrhead and to the works at Coplawhill. Among withdrawals during this period were the first 'Cunarder' to be taken out of service – No 1390 – and the prototype 'Coronation' No 1142. The last of the ex-Liverpool cars, No 1036, was withdrawn in July 1960; No 1055, which had been used by a group from Liverpool University for a tour on 21 February 1960, was, however, secured for preservation. Other notable withdrawals during this period included single-deck car No 1089, taken out of service on 9 August 1960 as a result of new regulations on standing passengers, and ex-driver training car No 1017.

On 30 January 1960, 'Coronation' No 1258 is seen at Park Road with a service on route 3; this service was converted to bus operation six months later, on 4 June 1960. Hamish Stevenson/Online Transport Archive (1569)

'Standard' No 506 is pictured at Bridgeton on 5 September 1959 with a route 10 service heading to Bridgeton Cross. Route 10 was converted to bus operation on 4 June 1960. Hamish Stevenson/Online Transport Archive (1379)

One of two routes converted to bus operation on 5 November 1960 was the 23 from Baillieston to Maryhill; on 6 April 1958 'Coronation' No 1291 stands at Baillieston with a service to Maryhill. John Meredith/Online Transport Archive (394/1)

'Coronation' No 1185 stands at the Elmvale Street, Springburn, terminus of route 16 on 6 June 1959; the service was cut back from this point to Keppochhill Road on 6 September 1959. The service from Keppochhill Road to Scotstoun was converted to bus operation on 11 March 1961. Hamish Stevenson/Online Transport Archive (999)

The last conversions in 1960 occurred on 6 November when route 23 was converted to bus operation and route 29 cut back from Tollcross to Broomhouse. The last cars on route 23 were No 1223 from Maryhill and No 1263 from Baillieston. By the end of 1960 only nine 'Standard' cars remained in service: Nos 17, 76 and 1051 at Partick, Nos 108/69, 283, 500/26/85 at Dalmarnock and No 176 in use as a shunter at Coplawhill. In addition, No 22 was in use as a shunter at Maryhill and Nos 156 and 556 retained as snowploughs at Maryhill.

The first conversion of 1961 occurred on 11 March when route 16 succumbed; the last car from Keppochhill Road, running to Partick depot, was 'Cunarder' No 1296. Also withdrawn at this stage were the shipyard specials that operated between Maryhill and Whiteinch; the last of these ran at 5.50 pm on 10 March 1961, operated by 'Coronation' No 1170. This closure should have resulted in the final withdrawal of the 'Standard' cars but fate intervened.

No 1005, by this date converted into a conventional double-ended car, stands at the terminus at Whiteinch on 5 August 1959. Whiteinch was the terminus of the shipyard specials from Maryhill that ceased to operate on 11 March 1961. Hamish Stevenson/ Online Transport Archive (1229)

Fire broke out at Dalmarnock depot at 1 am on 21 March 1961. This was not the first depot fire to have affected Glasgow but was by far the most destructive, with some 50 cars destroyed. The losses included five of the surviving 'Standard' cars – Nos 108/69, 283, 500/26 – as well as 19 'Coronations' and 26 'Cunarders'. No 1202 was damaged but repaired. The immediate consequence was that all the cars withdrawn following the conversion of route 16 were reinstated and a number of vintage cars withdrawn, but scheduled for preservation, were pressed back into service; these were Nos 488, 1088/89/115. In addition, No 1163, which had been withdrawn, was repaired and returned to service. Eventually, the corporation received an insurance payment of £200,000 for the loss; this was used to purchase additional buses. Between the fire and the next conversions only three cars were scrapped – Nos 1093/113/291.

'Standard' No 75 heads along Argyle Street with a route 18 service towards Springburn on 31 July 1959; the 18 and 18A were both converted to bus operation on 3 June 1961. Hamish Stevenson/ Online Transport Archive (1196)

The next abandonment occurred on 3 June when routes 18 and 18A were converted to bus operation; at the same time route 26 ceased to serve Burnside with all cars terminating at Farme Cross. The last cars on route 18 were No 488 from Springburn and No 1196 from Burnside; the last car from Burnside was No 1203 on route 26. The result of this conversion was that all the trams reprieved following the Dalmarnock

fire were again withdrawn. Two of the surviving 'Standard' cars – Nos 556 and 1051 – were quickly scrapped with No 76 taking over the duties as Coplawhill works shunter. By this date only four of the 'Kilmarnock Bogies' – Nos 1100/06/15/33 – remained and the withdrawal of the pre-war 'Coronation' cars was running at three a week by the autumn of the year.

Route 29 from Maryhill to Tollcross was converted on 21 October 1961; on 18 December 1959, ex-Liverpool No 1016 is pictured at Maryhill Park.
Hamish Stevenson/Online Transport Archive (1531)

The final abandonments of 1961 occurred on 21 October when route 29 was converted to bus operation and route 26 cut back from Farme Cross to Dalmarnock without replacement; the latter represented the last tram operation in Rutherglen. The last cars on route 29 were No 1215 from Tollcross and No 1241 from Maryhill; Maryhill depot closed at the same time with No 1222 being the last car to depart. The final tram from Farme Cross to Dalmarnock was No 1224.

The first route converted in 1962 was that from Anderston Cross to Baillieston – the 15 – which succumbed on 10 March; here, on 28 November 1959, 'Coronation' No 1231 is pictured on Rowchester Street with a service heading towards Parkhead. Hamish Stevenson/Online Transport Archive (1522)

At the end of 1961 the Glasgow system entered its final year; as if symbolically the last salt wagons were withdrawn at the end of the winter – the system would not survive long enough to see another. The first conversion of 1962 occurred on 10 March 1962 and saw route 15 converted to bus operation; the last tram from Anderston Cross was No 1242 at 11.40 pm; it arrived at Baillieston at 12.17 am. It departed Baillieston at 12.12 am for Dalmarnock depot, arriving there at 1 am, 15 minutes late. This left only two operational routes: the 9 and the 26. The first of these to succumb was route 26 on 2 June 1962. The last car to and from Dalmarnock was No 1318, departing the terminus for the last time at 12.6 am. No 1270, preceded by a piper, was the last car to enter Partick depot; the depot itself closed the following day with its surviving trams transferred to Dalmarnock.

'Standard' No 681 heads along Dalmarnock Road towards Burnside with a route 26 service. The section between Farme Cross and Burnside was abandoned on 3 June 1961 and services were curtailed from Farme Cross to Dalmarnock on 22 October 1961. The 26 was destined to be Glasgow's penultimate tram route, surviving until 2 June 1962. Hamish Stevenson/ Online Transport Archive (1061)

On 31 October 1959 two 'Kilmarnock Bogies' – Nos 1112 and 1133 – are seen on Dumbarton Road heading towards Dalmuir West on route 9; this was destined to be the last service in Glasgow, finally being converted to bus operation on 4 September 1962. Hamish Stevenson/ Online Transport Archive (1489)

D 9144

6d

Auchen-shuggle

Maukin-fauld Road

Maukin-fauld Road

1277 London Road

1277 London Road

Fraser Street

Fraser Street

Bridgeton Cross

Bridgeton Cross

Kent Street

Kent Street

Queen Street

Queen Street

Anderston Cross

GLASGOW CORPORATION TRANSPORT

Ticket available only on Tram on which it was issued. NOT TRANSFERABLE.

Issued subject to Bye-laws.

Glasgow Numerical Ptg. Co. Ltd.

1894 – 1962

FAREWELL TO GLASGOW'S TRAMS
1894 – 1962

LAST TRAM SOUVENIR TICKET

ANDERSTON CROSS and AUCHENSHUGGLE
2nd, 3rd and 4th SEPTEMBER, 1962

1894 – 1962

The scene was now set for the final closure, bringing to an end the story of 90 years of tramway operation in Glasgow. The final day of normal public service was 1 September with the last service car from Auchenshuggle to Dalmuir West being No 1383, which arrived at its destination at 11.26; it departed from Dalmuir West at 11.33 pm. At Yoker it was joined by No 1313, which bore the message 'The end of the greatest British tramway', at 11.52 pm. The two cars reached Dalmarnock at 12.55 am.

Following this there were special commemorative services between Anderston Cross and Auchenshuggle on 2 September (noon to 10 pm), 3 September (noon to 10 pm) and 4 September (noon to 5 pm) on which special 6d souvenir tickets were issued. The services were provided on the 2nd by Nos 1151/74/81/88/219/40/43/85, on the Monday by Nos 1151/74/88/219/240/43/85/308 and on the Tuesday by Nos 1174/88, 219/40/43/85/339/60. The last car in service on the Tuesday was No 1174, which left Anderston Cross at 4.50 pm, Auchenshuggle at 5.32 pm and, via Bridgeton Cross, reached Dalmarnock

depot at 6 pm. This was followed by the formal closure procession that included, on order of appearance, horse tram No 543 and electric cars Nos 672, 1089, 779, 1088, 1173/274/392/1172/262/82/83/97/352/63/82/85/147/367/79. This was, however, not quite the end as, on Thursday, 6 September, No 1282 operated a final journey in Clydebank.

At closure there were 62 trams based at Dalmarnock; following closure, these were moved under their own power between 11 September and 15 September to Coplawhill for disposal; the 'honour' of being the last car to make this fateful journey was 'Coronation' No 1163. By this date, work had already commenced on the removal of track from Auchenshuggle. Thus ended the story of Scotland's largest tramway system. Fortunately, a number of Glasgow trams have survived in preservation, both in their home city and elsewhere, helping to ensure future generations will still be able to experience a 'Standard' or 'Coronation' car, for example.

To mark the end of tramway operation in Glasgow, the transport department issued special tickets for use on the Anderston Cross to Auchenshuggle services on 2-4 September 1962. This is the front and reverse of one of these special tickets. Author's collection

Glasgow Depots

As might be expected with a fleet the size of Glasgow's, a number of depots accommodated the trams. The main workshops were located at Coplawhill; these continued to handle tram repairs through to final closure on 4 September 1962. Other depots were (in order of closure): Langside, located off Holmlea Road, ceased to be a tram depot on 29 September 1956 (with its cars transferred to Newlands for routes 5, 5A and 24 and to Govan for route 12); Jackson Street, Coatbridge, was acquired by the corporation following the takeover of operations in Airdrie and Coatbridge on 1 January 1922 and survived until the withdrawal of services beyond the city boundary into Airdrie on 4 November 1956; Elderslie, one of the depots that Glasgow inherited from Paisley District Tramways Co and located adjacent to the Elderslie terminus, closed on 11 May 1957 with the cessation of tramway operation in Paisley; Govan, built on Brand Street, was converted for trolleybus operation and lost its tram allocation on 15 November 1958 but was used for the storage of trams for scrap until 28 February 1959 (the last cars to leave were the 'Lightweight'

cars No 6, 1001); Possilpark, constructed at the junction of Hawthorn Street and Ashfield Road, ceased to be a tram depot on 7 June 1959; Newlands, built at the end of Newlandsfield Road on the route towards Rouken Glen, was hit by fire on 11 April 1948, in which a number of trams were damaged or destroyed, and survived until 4 June 1960 and closed with the conversion of the routes from Moss Park to Park Road, Kelvinbridge and Kelvinside to London Road; Dennistoun, sited just off Duke Street close to the Dennistoun terminus, closed on 5 November 1960 with the conversion of routes 23 and 29; Maryhill, situated on the west of the route north to Milngavie near Maryhill station, closed on 21 October 1961 with the closure of the route from Maryhill to Tollcross; Partick, built on Hayburn Street, lost its tram allocation on 2 June 1962 with the abandonment of the Clydebank-Dalmarnock service; Dalmarnock, located off Dalmarnock Road near Bridgeton Cross, was the location of the disastrous depot fire of 22 March 1961, which destroyed a large number of trams and severely damaged the building, but which survived until 9 September 1962.

Glasgow Closures

28 August 1948	29 – Uddingston-Broomhouse
23 January 1949	10 – Oatlands-Townhead
20 February 1949	2 – Polmadie-Provanmill / 19 – Springburn-Netherlee
2 April 1949	28 – Glenfield-Cross Stobs
3 December 1949	28 – Duntocher-Clydebank
1 July 1951	11 – Sinclair Drive-Milngavie
2 December 1951	24 – Kelvingrove-Sinclair Drive
15 June 1952	9 – cut back from Carmyle to Causewayside station
4 July 1953	5 – Clarkston-Holmlea Road
2 August 1953	32 – cut back from Bishopbriggs to Springburn
10 October 1954	23 – cut back from Airdrie to Baillieston
7 August 1955	Shawfield-Rutherglen
29 September 1956	14 – Cross Stobs-Arden
3 November 1956	15 – Airdrie-Baillieston / 17 – Eastfield-Cambuslang / 29 – Milngavie-Maryhill / 40 – Maryhill-Ibrox / Dumbreck

11 May 1957	4 – Renfrew-Hillington Road / 21 – Elderslie
	27 – Renfrew-Hillington Road / 28 – Renfrew Ferry-Glenfield
16 November 1957	5/5A – Holmlea Road-Kelvinside
15 March 1958	24 – Anniesland-Langside / 27 – Hillington Road / Shieldhall-Springburn
14 June 1958	7 – Bellahouston-Millerston
6 September 1958	4 – Hillington Road-Springburn
15 November 1958	12 – Mount Florida-Paisley Road Toll / 17 – Anniesland-Farme Cross
	22 – Crookston-Lambhill / 32 – Crookston-Bishopbriggs
14 March 1959	8 – Millerston-Rouken Glen
2 May 1959	33 – Springburn circular
6 June 1959	25 – Bishopbriggs-Carnwardic / Rouken Glen
6 September 1959	16 – cut back from Springburn to Keppochhill Road
31 October 1959	6 – Scotstoun-Alexandra Park / 14 – Kelvingrove-Arden
5 December 1959	31 – Lambhill-Merrylee
12 March 1960	1 – Dalmarnock-Dalmuir / 30 – Dalmarnock-Blairdairdie
4 June 1960	3 – Moss Park-Park Road Kelvinbridge / 10 – Kelvinside-London Road
6 November 1960	23 – Baillieston-Maryhill / 29 – Tollcross-Broomhouse
10 March 1961	16 – Scotstoun-Keppochhill Road
3 June 1961	18 – Springburn-Burnside / 18A – Springburn-Shawfield
21 October 1961	26 – cut back from Farme Cross to Dalmarnock
	29 – Maryhill-Tollcross
10 March 1962	15 – Anderston Cross-Baillieston
2 June 1962	26 – Clydebank-Dalmarnock
4 September 1962	9 – Dalmuir West-Auchenshuggle

Glasgow Fleet
1-5, 7-14/16-141/44-50/52-345/47-95/97-678/80-737/9-44/46-48/51-61/63-82/84/86-94/796-820/22-35/37-68/70-86/88-93/95/97-901/03-06/08-11/14-22/27-31/34-36/38-48/50/51/54-56/58-65/67-70/73/74/77/80-1000/39/40/50/51/88

The Glasgow 'Standard' class was numerically the second largest type of tram to operate in Britain. Built between 1898 and 1924, all had bodies supplied by the corporation with the exception of Nos 901-80 – GR&CW – fitted on Brill 21E four-wheel trucks. The early cars were open-top and unvestibuled with later ones fitted with top covers but, over the type's long life, the vast majority were rebuilt as fully enclosed between 1928 and 1935. Early post-war withdrawals occurred in 1946, and others – Nos 27, 334, 409 and 643 – were rebuilt after the war. Final withdrawals occurred in 1962 with a number temporarily reprieved due to the losses suffered in the Dalmarnock Depot fire in March 1961. Nos 22, 488, 585, 779, 812 and 1088 survive in preservation.

The single largest class of tramcar to survive in the British Isles after the Second World War was represented by the Glasgow 'Standard' class. Built over a near 30-year period and much modernised over their lives, examples of the type survived until the very end of tramway operation in the city. No 602, seen here at Scotstoun on 24 March 1949, dated originally from 1901 and survived in service until 1958. Michael H. Waller

Glasgow No 143, seen here at Paisley Road Toll on 22 February 1959, was one of the two 'Standard' cars rebuilt during the Second World War. Work on it was completed in February 1944; the other, No 679, was completed in June 1943. Hamish Stevenson/Online Transport Archive (174)

27, 143, 334, 409, 643/79

Two 'Standard' cars – Nos 143 and 679 – were rebuilt in 1944 and 1943 respectively. They had bodies supplied by the corporation itself and were fitted with Brill 21E trucks. The two lasted until 1958 (No 679) and 1959 (No 143). A further four cars – Nos 27, 334, 409, 643 – were rebuilt after the war, between May 1946 and February 1949. This quartet was withdrawn between February 1959 and November 1960.

821/36, 923/26/75

These five cars were originally built as normal Glasgow 'Standard' class double-deckers dating to 1900. They were built with bodies supplied by either the corporation itself or by GR&CW on Brill 21E four-wheel trucks. They were cut down in 1939 for use on the Duntocher route and survived in service until 1950.

1009/11-13/15-19/22-24

These 13 single-deck trams were acquired along with the Paisley District Tramways in 1923. Originally Paisley District Nos 9, 11-13, 15-19 and 22-24, they were built as open-top double-deck cars in 1904 with BEC bodies on Brush AA four-wheel trucks. Nos 1009-19/22-24/27/37/38 were cut down to single-deckers during 1924 and 1925 for use on the Duntocher route; Nos 1012/14/37/38 were withdrawn before 1945, and the remainder were withdrawn with the abandonment of the Duntocher route in 1949. No 1017 was subsequently used as a driver training car and was then preserved. No 1016 also survives but is a long-term restoration project and consists of little more than a kit of parts at the time of writing.

One of the five 'Standard' cars rebuilt as single-deckers is seen at the Duntocher terminus on 24 March 1949 in the company of other cars, including ex-Paisley No 1013.
Michael H. Waller

No 1022 was one of a number of trams acquired by Glasgow from Paisley District in 1923. It and a number of other ex-Paisley cars were cut down to single-deck for operation on the Duntocher route and were taken out of service when that service was withdrawn in 1949. No 1022 is seen in Clydebank on 24 March 1949, some nine months before withdrawal.
Michael H. Waller

Apart from ex-Paisley District cars that had been cut down to single-deck for use on the Duntocher route, a further 20 ex-Paisley cars remained in service in 1945 – Nos 1053-1072 – that dated originally to 1912-19. With the exception of No 1068 – seen here at Millerston on 23 March 1949 – all were withdrawn by 1953; No 1068 was kept at Elderslie until 1954 but no longer used in service and was subsequently preserved.
Michael H. Waller

1053-72

This batch of 20 trams was delivered new to Paisley District as Nos 53-72 between 1907 and 1920. They were acquired by Glasgow Corporation along with the Paisley District system in 1923 and renumbered 1053-72. When new they were fitted with Brush open-top (Nos 53-62) or Hurst Nelson open-top (Nos 63-72) bodies. Nos 53-62 were originally equipped with Brush trucks: 21E on Nos 53-58 and AA on Nos 59-62. Nos 63-72 were fitted with Hurst Nelson solid-forged trucks. All were rebuilt as fully enclosed cars on Brush 21E trucks between 1924 and 1931. All of the type were withdrawn between 1951 and 1953 with the exception of No 1068; this car was preserved upon withdrawal and has been restored as Paisley No 68.

1089

This was an experimental high-speed single-deck car supplied originally in 1926. The body was built at Coplawhill with 77E1 maximum traction bogies supplied by Brill. Its body was modified in 1932. Between then and 1949 the car operated on the Duntocher service; stored between 1949 and 1951, it was then used on John Brown shipyard works' services following the removal of its seats along one side (making the capacity 20 seated and 38 standing) until withdrawal in 1960. Restored to service after the Dalmarnock fire, it was preserved following final closure.

Glasgow No 1089 was destined to be a unique car; designed for high-speed running – up to 30mph – in competition with privately operated buses on longer-distance routes, the car was nicknamed 'Baillie Burt's Car', or 'Wee Baldy', as it had nothing on top, after the convener of the Tramways Committee at the time of its construction, Peter Burt, who proposed a number of the car's features. Restored to service briefly following the fire in Dalmarnock Depot in March 1961, No 1089 – seen here at Clydebank – featured in the closure procession in September 1962 and was subsequently preserved. Harry Luff/Online Transport Archive

142, 1090-1140

The 'Kilmarnock Bogies' were based upon two prototype cars – Nos 142 and 1090 – that were fitted with Hurst Nelson maximum traction bogies; the production batch had bogies supplied by the Kilmarnock Engineering Co. Bodies were supplied by Coplawhill (Nos 142 and 1090), Hurst Nelson (Nos 1091-1120), R. Y. Pickering (Nos 1121-30) and Brush (Nos 1131-40). The cars were delivered between 1927 and 1930. No 1100 was rebuilt as a streamlined car in 1941. All were withdrawn between 1959 and 1961 with the exception of Nos 142 (withdrawn 1954), 1100 (1962), 1109 (1954) and 1128 (1952). Nos 1100 and 1115 were preserved following withdrawal.

1141/42

These were the two prototype cars built for the development of the 'Coronation' class. Both were fitted with bodies built in Coplawhill but No 1141, built in 1936, had EMB Lightweight bogies, and No 1142, delivered the following year, had M&T equal-wheel bogies. The latter was painted in a special livery to mark the 1937 Coronation of King George VI. No 1142 was rebuilt after slight damage in 1940 and No 1141 was damaged but repaired, as a result of the Newlands Depot fire of 1948. Between 1945 and 1952, No 1142 operated with resilient wheels. No 1141 was withdrawn in 1961 and No 1142 the previous year.

One of the 'Kilmarnock Bogies', No 1114, is seen heading through Clydebank on 24 March 1949. Nos 1091-1140 were fitted with maximum traction bogies supplied by Kilmarnock Engineering Co. Michael H. Waller

In 1936 and 1937 two prototype streamlined cars – Nos 1141 and 1142 respectively – were produced as experimental cars. No 1141 was damaged as a result of the fire at Newlands Depot and is seen here on track used by the Permanent Way Department adjacent to the Works at Coplawhill on 10 August 1952. Michael H. Waller

1143-1292

The 150 members of the 'Coronation' class were delivered between 1936 and 1941 with bodies built at Coplawhill on EMB Lightweight bogies. Nos 1168/220 were rebuilt after fires in 1938 and 1942 respectively. No 1275 was rebuilt after wartime damage in 1941. The upper deck of 1163 was also rebuilt in 1941 and No 1178 was rebuilt in 1944. Two trams – Nos 1148/239 – were rebuilt after the Newlands Depot fire but Nos 1153/56/204/07/08/10/14/16/27/29/33/44/51 were destroyed in the fire at Dalmarnock Depot. All survivors were withdrawn between 1959 and 1962 with Nos 1173/245/74/82 preserved. No 1147 was the last Glasgow tram scrapped.

Between 1936 and 1941, no fewer than 150 'Coronation' class bogie cars were supplied with corporation-built bodies on EMB Lightweight bogies. Here No 1243 is seen on Tollcross Road on 23 March 1949. Michael H. Waller

One of the quartet of four-wheel experimental cars built during 1939 and 1940, No 1002 is pictured at Millerston on 22 March 1949.
Michael H. Waller

1001-1004, 6

Nos 1001-04 were a quartet of experimental four-wheel cars built during 1939 and 1940. All four had bodies supplied by Coplawhill; Nos 1001/02 had four-wheel trucks supplied by M&T, and Nos 1003/04 had EMB trucks. Nos 1001/03 received reconditioned trucks from Nos 97 and 413 respectively. All four trams were withdrawn in 1959. No 6 was built following the same design in 1943 to replace 'Standard' No 6 that had been destroyed by enemy action during the Second World War on 13 March 1941.

No 6 was damaged in the Newlands Depot fire of 1948 but was rebuilt and remained in service until 1959.

1005

No 1005 was an experimental single-ended car completed in 1947 with a body supplied by Coplawhill fitted on M&T HS44 bogies. The car, when new, was finished in a non-standard blue livery and was equipped with VAMBAC electrical control. The car was first used to carry passengers on 4 September 1947 for a tour of the system by Dutch enthusiasts. It entered regular service on route 33 (the Springburn-Charing Cross circular) on 22 December 1947. In early 1948 it was modified by the provision of an interlock to prevent it being driven while the air brakes were still applied. The car was modified to operate with rear entrance and front exit in 1949, reappearing in fleet livery, and had its VAMBAC control equipment replaced with normal electrical equipment two years later. In 1956 No 1005 was converted to double-ended; the car survived until withdrawal in 1962. One bogie was preserved for display in the transport museum.

Pictured when new in its unique blue livery at Newlands Depot on 19 June 1949, No 1005 was constructed as a single-ended bogie car. Fitted with VAMBAC control equipment, the car was soon repainted in the more usual green, orange and white livery and, in 1956, was converted into a double-ended car.
Michael H. Waller

'Cunarder' No 1293, the first of the 100 post-war trams acquired by Glasgow of this type, stands at Millerston on 23 March 1949, shortly after its delivery and still appears to be in pristine condition. No 1293 was one of the many cars destroyed in the disastrous Dalmarnock Depot fire. Michael H. Waller

1293-1392

The single largest batch of trams delivered in the post-war years was represented by the 100-strong 'Cunarder' or 'Coronation II' type delivered between 1948 and 1952. Again fitted with bodies supplied by Coplawhill, the trams were equipped with M&T 596 equal-wheel bogies. On 1 April 1949 the general manager proposed that ten of the cars be built as single-deckers; this proposal was rejected by the Transport Committee on 12 April. Nos 1316/23-26/33-35/37/44-47/53/54/57/65/68-70/76/86-88/91 were destroyed in the Dalmarnock fire. The remainder were all withdrawn between 1960 and 1962. Two examples – Nos 1297 and 1392 – were preserved.

In 1954 and 1955 Glasgow constructed eight replacement 'Coronation' cars; six of these, of which No 1395 seen at the Albert Drive and Shields Road crossing on route 3, were funded by insurance following the Newlands Fire. Of these six, four, including No 1395, were eventually destroyed in the disastrous fire at Dalmarnock Depot in March 1961.
John Meredith/Online Transport Archive (393/11)

1393-98, 1255/79

The first six of these eight cars were replacement 'Coronation' cars constructed in 1954 with the insurance money covering the vehicles lost in the Newlands Depot fire. With bodies constructed at Coplawhill, Nos 1393-98 were initially fitted with EMB Lightweight bogies acquired second-hand from Liverpool, although a number were subsequently retrucked with standard Glasgow equipment in 1961. The body of No 1279 was a replacement one constructed late in 1954 to replace the car's second body following the latter's destruction in a fire at Renfrew Ferry on 26 April 1954, and No 1255 received a replacement body – the last to be constructed – in 1955 following the destruction of its original body in a fire at Coplawhill Works on 25 February 1955. It was the second time that No 1279's body had been destroyed by fire; it had at Giffnock on 26 November 1948, entering service with its second body on 2 July 1951. It had also been damaged during the Blitz of 1941; clearly it was not a lucky car! Nos 1393/95-97 were destroyed in the Dalmarnock Depot fire; the remainder were all withdrawn during 1961 and 1962.

1006-16/18-38/41-49/52-56

In 1953/54 Glasgow took advantage of the rapid abandonment of the Liverpool system to acquire 47 streamlined bogie cars that had originally been built during 1936 and 1937. The trams acquired were Liverpool Nos 942/34/38/35/30/31 /23/28/32/40/21/22/26/37/36/18/ 39/27/25/41/24/33/29/19, 899, 901, 881/85, 902, 891/880/83/78/86, 903 874/77/75/71/87/93/97/84/90/69 and 904 respectively. Although all had Liverpool-built bodies, Nos 1006/18-38/41-49 were fitted with M&T Swing link bogies; the remainder were supplied with EMB Lightweight or Heavyweight bogies. The second-hand cars were withdrawn in Glasgow between 1957 and 1960; No 1055 (ex-Liverpool 869) was preserved following withdrawal.

During 1953 and 1954 Glasgow acquired 46 of the streamlined bogie cars then being withdrawn in Liverpool. No 1015 is seen at Tollcross on 22 May 1954. The ex-Liverpool cars were destined for a relatively short life in Scotland, being withdrawn between 1957 and 1960 as the Glasgow network rapidly contracted. Michael H. Waller

Works cars

To operate the system, Glasgow Corporation employed a significant number of dedicated works cars. The fleet comprised both vehicles built specifically for works duties and cars converted from redundant passenger cars. The final conversion undertaken was on 'Standard' No 722, which was converted into a tool van (No 40) following withdrawal in 1954. Of the works fleet, two examples were preserved: Mains Department No 1, a cable-laying car that dated originally to 1901, and tools van No 21. Both of these are part of the National Tramway Museum collection. Tool van No 22 was also acquired by the Tramway Museum Society, but dismantled and its truck used in the restoration of 'Standard' No 22.

Three of Glasgow's extensive fleet of works cars are pictured at Barrland Street Yard with No 29 closest to the camera. This was a tool van, one of seven, Nos 26-32, converted from redundant ex-Paisley cars during 1933 and 1934. No 29 had been originally passenger car No 1007 (ex-Paisley No 7), which dated originally to 1904.
R. W. A. Jones/Online Transport Archive (GL32)

PRESERVATION

A number of Scottish trams survive in preservation, although many more might have survived had the preservation movement been stronger in the mid-1950s; the story of post-war Scottish operators is that a number of prime examples of trams suitable for preservation succumbed to scrapping.

Of the four post-war fleets, Glasgow is by far the best represented. The newly opened Museum of Transport possesses a number of cars. Apart from horse tram No 543, there are the following electric trams: 'Room & Kitchen' car No 672, 'Standard' class Nos 779 and 1088, single-deck car No 1089, 'Coronation' class No 1173 and 'Cunarder' No 1392. The National Tramway Museum at Crich possesses the single-largest collection of ex-Glasgow trams. These are 'Standard' class Nos 22 and 812, 'Kilmarnock Bogies' Nos 1100/15, 'Coronation' class No 1282, 'Cunarder' class No 1297, Mains Department No 1 and tool van No 22. In addition, the National Tramway Museum also hosts two trams that operated in Glasgow: ex-Paisley District No 68 (1068) and ex-Liverpool No 869 (1055). There are two ex-Glasgow trams at the Summerlee Museum at Coatbridge; these are one of the ex-Paisley trams cut down to single deck for use on the Duntocher route

Glasgow 'Standard' No 1088 on display in the new Museum of Transport in the city. No 1088, delivered in June 1924, was the last Glasgow 'Standard' car to be built and survived in service until June 1961. Author's collection

Glasgow Standard
No 22 is one of two 'Standard' cars preserved at the National Tramway Museum. It has been restored to the condition in which it was delivered in 1922 with an open-balcony top. Vintage Carriages Trust/Online Transport Archive (7120)

(No 1017) and a 'Coronation' car (No 1245). The body of ex-Paisley No 1016, sister to No 1017 and deemed a long-term restoration project, was also stored at Summerlee for a number of years but, at the time of writing, is housed at the Glasgow Bus Museum. 'Standard' class No 585 is part of the collection of the Science Museum. There were two Glasgow trams exported for preservation abroad. 'Standard' No 488 moved to Paris; however, this car has now been repatriated to the UK and is, at the time of writing, undergoing restoration at the Ffestiniog Railway before being moved to the East Anglian Transport Museum near Lowestoft. It is anticipated that the car will enter service there in mid-2016. 'Coronation' car No 1274 was exported to the Seashore Trolley Museum at Kennebunkport in the US, where it remains.

Of the Edinburgh fleet, only one electric car – No 35 – was preserved at the time;

this is now on display at the National Tramway Museum. A horse car, No 23, has recently been fully restored and is now on display at Lathalmond, and the body of a cable car converted for use with overhead, No 226, is undergoing restoration. A number of other lower-deck bodies are also extant.

In terms of Aberdeen, a horse tram, No 1, of the Aberdeen District Tramways can be seen at the Grampian Transport Museum at Alford but no electric car was preserved. No Dundee electric tram survived closure, although steam trailer No 21 has been restored and is on display at the National Tramway Museum. The bodies of two further steam trailers – Nos 2 and 22 – are awaiting restoration. Beyond these, there are a couple of preserved trams from operators that ceased before the Second World War. At Summerlee can be seen Lanarkshire Tramways Co No 53, an open-top car dating originally to 1908, and at the

Grampian Transport Museum, Cruden Bay No 2 is on display. The latter was one of two single-deck cars built by the Great North of Scotland Railway in 1899 for use on its short tramway; withdrawn in 1940, the two were rescued in 1988 and one car rebuilt from the surviving parts. One of the 1931-built Falkirk cars, No 14, was restored utilising trucks that had once operated on the 4ft 0in-gauge Glasgow Subway. The car is now in the custodianship of Falkirk Museums.

Beyond these, there remain a number of bodies in varying degrees of decay known to preservationists; whether any of these bodies will be acquired and restored in the future is uncertain.

There is only one operating heritage tramway in Scotland – that at Summerlee – which houses the two ex-Glasgow cars (Nos 1017/245) detailed earlier and the ex-Lanarkshire No 53. Also in operational use at the museum is an ex-Dusseldorf single-deck car, No 392, that dates to 1950. The Summerlee museum, which first operated trams on 1 April 1988, uses standard-gauge track, thus both the Glasgow trams have been regauged (No 1245 was, in fact, regauged during its sojourn at the East Anglian Transport Museum before its return north).

Not strictly preservation, although it did feature the operation of preserved trams, the Glasgow Garden Festival, which ran from 26 April to 26 September 1988, saw a number of trams operate within the festival site. These included Paisley No 68 and Glasgow No 1297. The operation represented the first trams to run in the city since September 1962.

Now part of the National Collection and based at Crich, Edinburgh No 35 was for a number of years based at Blackpool and was used in service. It is seen here at Talbot Square, Blackpool, on 29 September 1985, during the celebrations held that year to mark the centenary of electric tramcar operation in the town.
Michael H. Waller

BIBLIOGRAPHY

British & Irish Tramway Systems since 1945; Michael H. Waller and Peter Waller; Ian Allan Publishing, Shepperton; 1992

Edinburgh's Transport; D. L. G. Hunter; Advertiser Press; 1964

Glasgow Trams: 40 Years On; Ian Stewart; Scottish Tramway & Transport Society; 2002

Lanarkshire's Trams; Alan Brotchie; NB Traction; 1993

Modern Tramway; Light Railway Transport League; 1945 onwards

Scottish Tramway Fleets; Alan W. Brotchie; NB Traction; 1968

The Directory of British Tram Depots; Keith Turner, Shirley Smith and Paul Smith; OPC; 2001

The Glasgow Tramcar; Ian Stewart; Scottish Tramway Museum Society; 1983

The Golden Age of Tramways; Charles F. Klapper; Routledge & Kegan Paul; 1961

The Rothesay Tramways Company 1879-1949; Ian L. Cormack; STTS; 1986

The Tramways of Eastern Scotland; J. C. Gillham & R. J. S. Wiseman; LRTA; undated

The Tramways of Western Scotland; J. C. Gillham & R. J. S. Wiseman; LRTA; undated

Tramway Memories: Edinburgh; George Fairley; Ian Allan Publishing; 2006

Tramway Review; Light Railway Transport League; 1950 onwards